Young John McGahern

Young John
McGahern

Becoming a Novelist

DENIS SAMPSON

OXFORD
UNIVERSITY PRESS

OXFORD

UNIVERSITY PRESS

Great Clarendon Street, Oxford ox2 6DP

Oxford University Press is a department of the University of Oxford.
It furthers the University's objective of excellence in research, scholarship,
and education by publishing worldwide in

Oxford New York

Auckland Cape Town Dar es Salaam Hong Kong Karachi
Kuala Lumpur Madrid Melbourne Mexico City Nairobi
New Delhi Shanghai Taipei Toronto

With offices in

Argentina Austria Brazil Chile Czech Republic France Greece
Guatemala Hungary Italy Japan Poland Portugal Singapore
South Korea Switzerland Thailand Turkey Ukraine Vietnam

Oxford is a registered trade mark of Oxford University Press
in the UK and in certain other countries

Published in the United States
by Oxford University Press Inc., New York

British Library Cataloguing in Publication Data

Data available

Library of Congress Cataloging in Publication Data

Data available

Typeset by SPI Publisher Services, Pondicherry, India
Printed in Great Britain
on acid-free paper by
Clays Ltd, St Ives plc

ISBN 978-0-19-964177-2

1 3 5 7 9 10 8 6 4 2

For the readers in my life:
my mother, aged 93, still a reader;
Gay; Conor, Bobby, and Anna;
Sophie and Meghan, readers all;
and Camille, Madeleine, and Nora,
still happy to have me read to them.

Preface

I first heard of John McGahern some weeks before *The Barracks* appeared in bookshops in March 1963. My English teacher, Augustine Martin, held up a copy of the Faber and Faber edition which he had received for review. I was lucky in my English teacher since much of his enthusiasm for current Irish writing flowed over into our classroom. He took a special interest in McGahern for they had both spent their childhoods in and around Ballinamore, County Leitrim, in the 1930s and 1940s. McGahern's mother had been his teacher for a while, and Martin knew the novelist a little in literary circles in Dublin—in the late 1950s, they had both studied English at University College Dublin and some years later frequented the home of Mary Lavin, the celebrated writer of short stories. Martin's excitement at this new novel arrested me: it conveyed his sense that literature captured in words a living reality and that one's own experience might be reflected and shaped in those words.

I did not discover the reality of McGahern's work for myself until I had left Ireland and was living in Canada in the 1970s. By then I could begin to appreciate its high artistic accomplishment and to understand something of how it was rooted in his earliest experiences in rural Ireland. I could read my own inner life and formation in *The Barracks*, *The Dark*, and in the stories of *Nightlines* that followed. I could recognize the rural culture that was reflected in them and the anguished voice that searched relentlessly for meaning and calm in bewildering personal circumstances. It was this recognition that drew me into searching for an appropriate way of appreciating the work and for an understanding of the literary traditions and models in which he had found inspiration and clarified his own place.

I was fortunate. In early 1979 I met John McGahern in Montreal with the intention of taping an interview. He had come to read at McGill University. I expected him to choose stories from the new volume, *Getting Through*, but instead he read from *The Pornographer*, scheduled to be published nine months later. He also spoke passionately about the essays of Proust, in particular 'Days of Reading', the

Preface Proust had written for his translation of John Ruskin's *Sesame and Lilies*. His rapt appreciation of Proust's account of the spiritual significance of solitary reading was as unexpected as the comic, multilayered style of the new novel. Our conversation the following morning prompted him to leave the typescript of the new novel with me. In some trepidation, I spent the weekend reading it and then returned it with a brief response. 'I was deeply moved that you should read the novel so carefully and so generously', he wrote back. 'It was mostly what I tried to do, what I half-hoped.' And then he invited me to visit him the following summer at his home in Leitrim where he had settled a few years earlier, not far from Ballinamore. That first exchange was the beginning of a friendship that lasted for the remainder of his life. Our meetings were intermittent, in Leitrim and elsewhere, but each year, at some stage, I would hear of work in progress or receive a typescript or a new publication, and I would give as careful a reading as I could to the new work. Few events were as exciting to me during those years as a new story or novel from McGahern: detecting the constant grain of his talent and the new artistic means he found to articulate it became an accompaniment to my own life.

My appreciation of his work and my search for understanding its nature and genesis have continued up to the present. Along the way, I wrote a book, *Outstaring Nature's Eye: The Fiction of John McGahern*, and many reviews and essays on particular works, including the last, *Memoir*. This 'unconventional autobiography', as he called it, his only book of non-fiction, situates his life up to about 1970 in the familial and social circumstances of his first decades. 'I think that a writer writes out of his private world,' he said a few years before he began to write the memoir, 'and that is more or less shaped by the time one is twenty, twenty-one or twenty-two. Everything that happens to you changes you, but that private world is essentially shaped and one always works on that.'[1] *Memoir* consists largely of an account of his relationships with his beloved mother, who died when he was nine, and his estranged father, who lived on until McGahern was in middle age. Much of what he tells is a record of trauma, brutality, and poverty, yet this is not the confessional narrative of a 'victim' or a 'survivor'. Rather, it partakes in the aesthetic project which was central from the beginning: 'to see and to celebrate even the totally intolerable'.[2] The narrative voice frames the 'intolerable' in a wise serenity, anchored, he seems to say, in the love of his mother in his earliest years and in the landscape of Leitrim where he settled for the second half of his life. Like the last novel, *That They May Face the Rising Sun*,[3] it incorporates a kind of pastoral, an ideal image which reflects the antithesis of the anguish, and perhaps morbidity, of the early novels. From an early and clear-eyed focus on death and suffering, these last books suggest, his vision of life had emphatically turned towards light and acceptance. That trajectory, so apparently simple when stated this way, was actually a whole life's search.

Memoir is the work of a poet in prose, and only the depth of feeling and insight allows us to understand how he became such a writer or renewed himself as an artist. Although it is a narrative of his life up to middle age, it is a family memoir, and not a portrait of the artist as a young man. As a context for this narrative, he includes an interpretation of the social, political, and religious forces that shaped rural life in Ireland in the decades of the mid-century. Apart from his discovery in adolescence of the magical experience of reading, it says little that might offer insight into how he discovered and nurtured his talent or how his distinctive vision and style came to be so mature in his mid-twenties, when he wrote *The Barracks*. In later decades McGahern often expressed distaste for the special privilege attached to the term artist, a sentimentality of a particular version of Romanticism, he felt, and so this silence in *Memoir* is not surprising. Just as he disliked the aura of heroism, he also disliked the notion of self-expression. And he insisted that his fiction was not autobiographical.

It is all the more surprising, then, that at the end of his life he wrote *Memoir*, for in it he reports at length on the familial material drawn on in the fiction, to confirm, as it were, that his art is, indeed, deeply self-referential. For instance, so many of the key incidents and images of his childhood passed in County Leitrim with his mother repeat those same details from Part I of *The Leavetaking*; in fact, the many pages that describe the traumatic parting from the mother, the exclusion of the children from the house, and the day of her funeral are reprinted unchanged as autobiography, thus blurring any easily demarcated boundary between fiction and non-fiction. McGahern did not comment on this, but later he explained that certain short stories are now excluded from *Creatures of the Earth: New and Selected Stories* and have been moved into *Memoir* where they really belong. It is also evident that *The Dark* and many of the father–son stories are solidly anchored in the experience of his own earlier life. And it is easy to see how closely the family narrative in *Amongst Women* corresponds to developments in the McGahern family during the 1950s and later. In the light of such revelations about his material, and with the insight into the process of the composition of the fiction that may be gleaned from the many drafts he preserved and deposited in the library of National University of Ireland Galway, McGahern's achievement can be seen in a new way.

Here, I have written a series of chapters on the decade before his first novel appeared, the 'years of training', as he called them, meaning his self-education as an artist. During these years, McGahern came to the firm conclusion that he had a vocation to become an artist, and set about discovering what that might mean in his case and how he might achieve it. It was a time of extensive reading and of new knowledge. He discovered those writers who would shape his thinking about artistic vision and technique; he clarified where he stood in relation to received religious, cultural, and political beliefs; and he clarified his own vision and his ideas about the character of the poet. In short, he established the intellectual foundation upon which the young writer could rely as he created his first novel. I believe that this foundation enabled him to gain distance from the authority of father and home, from the milieu in which he had to work as a teacher, and from entrenched perspectives on cultural identity and national history. Most of all, perhaps, it allowed him to clarify how his Catholic formation had permeated his moral and spiritual life, and how art and religious belief are related. His intensive reading of classic writers, which I alluded to in *Outstaring Nature's Eye*, and which I drew upon in formulating some of my readings of the novels and stories, I have now set out in a new way. My belief is that an understanding of his intellectual and artistic formation will add to an increased appreciation of the work of a lifetime.

I have been told by people who knew McGahern at the beginning of his career—and documentary evidence supports this view—that the main outlines of his thinking and his artistic orientation changed very little over the years. Writing with admiration of Flaubert, McGahern remarked, 'He seemed hardly to change at all in what, for that time, was a long life. He came on his central ideas very early and they served him till his death.'[4] In his own case, the fundamentals were in place by the early 1960s, and for the rest of his life, as he worked and reworked his material and renewed his art, those core convictions remained.

The material the novelist was given had to be imagined over and over as part of each new story or novel, so that what may appear at first to be repetition is actually part of a continuing process of self-definition in literary images, an unceasing search for its ultimate spiritual and literary meaning, the absolute reality of his experience. Seamus Heaney has said this best:

> McGahern's imagination is ruminant. It chews the cud of the past, digests and redigests it, interrogates it for its meaning, savours it for its bittersweet recurrence. This is the way to understand the compulsive return to certain landscapes and themes in his work . . . it would be a misunderstanding of his art to imply . . . that McGahern is repeating himself. He is rather retrieving himself, achieving a new self.[5]

Heaney's sympathetic insight in his review of *The Leavetaking* points to an essential pattern that encompasses much more than the material of McGahern's childhood self and his mother in that novel.

The recollection of deep and unmanageable feelings—images, as he often said, which came to him and would not go away—were the spur to his writing, and why he needed to write. The most common dramatic situation in the first half of his writing life grew out of this. In the story of the adolescent in *The Dark*, or of the woman dying of cancer in *The Barracks*, or stories of *Nightlines*, such as 'Wheels', 'Korea', or 'The Recruiting Officer', an individual bears a heavy truth of feeling and responsibility for his or her own life, isolated from anyone who would understand or love, and often, in fact, faced by antagonistic forces which would deny that reality of individual experience and repress the need to communicate it. It is a personal, a social, and a spiritual reality, and yet it is marked by a gap of incomprehension; this gap is what art tries to acknowledge and to bridge. The foundation of his literary career is here. Only in literary writing is such incomprehension overcome and honesty possible, the truth of the private world set out in trustworthy words.

W. B. Yeats, the poet to whose work McGahern often returned, declared in his first poem, 'Words alone are certain good'. McGahern's own version of this credo appears in a manuscript regarding the experience of writing:

> As in reading, when we become conscious that we are no longer reading romances or fables or adventure but versions of our own life, so it suddenly came to me that while I seemed to be playing with words in reality I was playing with my own life. And words, for me, have always been presences as well as meanings. Through words I could experience my own life with more reality than ordinary living.[6]

As McGahern worked, sentence by sentence, the moral force of 'good writing' would be his abiding faith, and in such writing he would discover the joy of imaginative release. At first, this imaginative release was found in reading, especially the solitary reading on a boat on Oakport Lake, and that freedom was soon associated with the life of the mind made available to him in school in Carrick-on-Shannon. Religious rituals and the rituals of art were also associated with it, until eventually he committed himself to his 'secret vocation' in Dublin. There he discovered modern art and ideas, in fiction, in the theatre, and in film. Having honed his literary style in *The Barracks*, he went on to remake it and to renew his faith in it throughout his lifetime. The formation of this artist is the mysterious process I attempt to trace and to appreciate in this book.

Acknowledgements

During the research and writing phase, I received help of various kinds from many people; their practical help was valuable, but their interest and encouragement were essential. I want to thank Mark Abley, Brendan Barrington, Neil Belton, Tom French, Lionel Gallagher, Neill Joy, John Kenny, Terence Killeen, Ann Murphy, Eoghan Ó Súilleabháin, Antoinette Quinn, Mary Shine Thompson, Colm Tóibín, Stanley van der Ziel, Caroline Walsh, Niall Walsh, Tony Whelan, and, as always, Gay Sampson. I owe a particular debt to a number of earlier readers of this manuscript for their strong endorsement of what I had accomplished; three editors at different publishers read the manuscript before it came to Oxford University Press, and I want to thank them especially for their commitment of time and energy to it, even though in the end they could not publish it. In one case, three anonymous readers also submitted reports, and their appreciation of it, as well as suggestions for improvement, were valuable responses in the later stages. In the beginning my first reader was George O'Brien, long-time friend, and in this case, as often, his broad encouragement included enough nuanced doubts to make me think again of the overall shape of what I was attempting to do. I would like to thank two individuals in particular. Patrick Gregory opened to me the private archive of materials related to the early stages of McGahern's career, which, to his surprise, he discovered in his attic; our subsequent correspondence and conversations were a source of delight and enlightenment. It was in Patrick Gregory's collection I found the photograph which appears on the front cover, and for this I owe him especial thanks. Without the interest and support of Declan Kiberd, I might never have committed time and energy to another major work on John McGahern, and I hope he and the others mentioned above are not disappointed by the result. Any limitations it may have, or errors of fact or interpretation, are entirely my responsibility.

Archivists and librarians at many institutions have helped me in this work, in some cases well beyond the call of duty, and I thank all of them: Kieran Hoare, Fergus Fahey and Vera Orschel, James Hardiman Library, NUI Galway; Robert Brown, Archives, Faber and Faber; Katharine Beutner, Harry Ransom Center, University of Texas, Austin; John Frederick, McPherson Library/Special Collections, University of Victoria, Canada; Seamus Helferty, UCD Archives, University College Dublin; Evelyn Flanagan, Special Collections, University College Dublin; John Killen, Linen Hall Library, Belfast; Gerard Lyne and Máire Ní Chonaláin, Department of Manuscripts Collections, National Library of Ireland; in addition, I have been helped by staff at the Manuscripts and Archives Division, New York Public Library; Dublin City Library; Lilly Library, University of Indiana; Howard Gotlieb Research Centre, Mugar Library, Boston University; and I have availed of the services of McGill University Library, Montreal, and the British Library, London.

More generally, I would like to thank the community of scholars who have engaged with my earlier writing about McGahern's work; from the reviewers of *Outstaring Nature's Eye* to those who have referred to it in the course of their own work, to editors of publications who included occasional later articles, to those who have contacted me directly over the years, I have drawn encouragement and been energized to continue my ruminations on the meaning and significance of McGahern's work. Long before this, however, I found energy and purpose in my friendship with the writer himself, and although we rarely talked about his own work, nor did he indicate very often that he had read something I had written about it, yet he too encouraged me to believe that what I was doing was worthwhile.

Jonathan Williams has been a staunch advocate of this manuscript in his work in finding a publisher, for which I owe him a great debt of thanks, and in his determination to cast his eagle eye over it again and again; this Welsh-Canadian-Irishman has saved me embarrassment many times in my handling of the English language and has endeavoured to educate me with his marginal comments: is St Jude the patron of 'hopeless cases' or 'hopeless causes'?

At Oxford, I would like to thank Hermione Lee, who read the manuscript at short notice and whose enthusiasm for it ensured its quick passage to acceptance by OUP. Jacqueline Baker's equal enthusiasm for it has made my work with the Press a pleasure from the beginning. In addition to offering her my thanks, I want to include all of her colleagues who worked to bring the book to the public.

My thanks to the following individuals and institutions for granting permission to use published and unpublished material:

Quotations from the published work of John McGahern are reprinted by permission of Faber and Faber.

Quotations from letters and unpublished manuscript drafts held in various archives and in private hands (© The Estate of John McGahern) reprinted by permission of A. M. Heath & Co Ltd.

The lines from six poems by Patrick Kavanagh are reprinted from *Collected Poems*, edited by Antoinette Quinn (Allen Lane, 2004) by kind permission of the Trustees of the Estate of the late Katherine B. Kavanagh, through the Jonathan Williams Literary Agency.

Kieran Hoare, Archivist, granted permission for the use of material in the John McGahern Papers held in Special Collections, James Hardiman Library, NUIG.

Quotations from letters to Patrick Swift are included by courtesy of Lilly Library, Indiana University, Bloomington, Indiana.

The Archives and Manuscripts Department, New York Public Library, permitted the use of correspondence in the *New Yorker* Records, Astor, Lenox and Tilden Foundations.

John Killen permitted the use of letters in the Michael McLaverty Papers, Linen Hall Library, Belfast.

John Frederick permitted the use of letters in the John Montague Papers, Special Collections, McPherson Library, University of Victoria, Canada.

Colette O'Daly permitted the use of letters in the Brian Friel Papers, Department of Manuscripts, National Library of Ireland, Dublin.

Tony Whelan permitted the use of letters in his private papers.

Contents

1

Pleasure and Knowledge

The pleasures and satisfactions of knowledge first came to John McGahern in his mid-teens, and the desire to pursue them arose from his own innate ability. School, for him, was not the same as for the others, as he makes clear in a late tribute to the Presentation Brothers who ran his secondary school in Carrick-on-Shannon: 'I look back on those five years as the beginning of an adventure that has not stopped. Each day I cycled towards Carrick was an anticipation of delights. The fear and drudgery of school disappeared; without realizing it, through the pleasures of the mind, I was beginning to know and to love the world.'[1] They were 'years of luck and privilege—and of grace, actual grace'. These were the years when he gained intellectual 'tools' and performed exceptionally well in examinations, ending with the top results in County Roscommon in his Leaving Certificate so that he won a scholarship to university and was also 'called to training' as a primary teacher. But they were also the years of Shakespeare, Wordsworth, and Tennyson, the required texts of his English syllabus, and of Dickens and other novelists, loaned to him by his English teacher. Frank Mannion, the teacher in question, was committed to introducing his students to the pleasures of reading and to teaching the recognition of those qualities that make for good and weak writing. While his teacher helped him awaken to language and literature as refined expression, it is evident that there was a more general awakening during his adolescence to the enabling power of knowledge, to the life of the mind.

The autobiographical account of this discovery of reading and knowledge as central, self-defining elements of the man and writer was written in the 1990s. The positive aura of delight, adventure, and love convey a powerful sense of freedom and

ease, the antithesis of the violence, fear, and repression he experienced at home in the barracks in Cootehall. The awakening to a
'love of the world' replaced 'the fear and drudgery of school', he
writes in retrospect, yet an earlier retrospect, the dramatization
of adolescence in *The Dark*, includes a vivid depiction of that 'fear
and drudgery'. That novel, which explores the shame and anxi-
eties of the brutalized young Mahoney, does not dramatize such
luxuries of the mind: in the struggle with his father, school results
will be his passport to a separate life. So much depends on his
academic success that education is a ground of both dread and
of fantasy:

> The University was a dream: not this slavish push in and out through
> wind and rain on a bicycle, this dry constant cramming to pass the
> exam, no time to pause to know and enjoy anything...The University
> would be different, you'd seen pictures, all stone with turrets sur-
> rounded by trees, walks between the lawns and trees, long golden
> evenings in the boats on the Corrib. You'd be initiated into
> mystery.[2]

But when he does succeed in his exams, and does win a scholarship
to the university, his first days in Galway extend the nightmare: he
experiences 'the shambles of a dream' and abandons the romantic
possibilities of higher education for a clerical job.

In deciding to leave the university, however, young Mahoney
comes to a firm resolution, and in this moment one senses that he
speaks for the author: 'One day, one day, you'd come perhaps to
more real authority than all this, an authority that had need of neither vast buildings nor professorial chairs nor robes nor solemn
organ tones, an authority that was simply a state of mind, a calm-
ness even in the face of the turmoil of your own passing.'[3] The bitterness and disillusionment that mark the humiliating withdrawal
from the university are surely appropriate for this fiction of a bereft
and impoverished adolescence. There is no happy ending here, no
hint that dreams are fulfilled. It is a fiction marked by epiphany and
irony, yet this narrative of young Mahoney's harsh beginning has
embedded in it a portrait of the artist as a young man. He does not
leave in triumph, determined to master his fate with 'silence, exile,
and cunning', but the author makes clear that the accomplishment

of the novel itself is the proof that such an inner 'authority' can be achieved, even in the least promising circumstances.

This is the kind of authority that was gradually won during the Dublin decade, 1953–64. When McGahern referred to 'my years of training in the secret Dublin years', he meant not only intellectual training—the development of the 'tools' given him by the Presentation Brothers, or the extent of his education in St Patrick's Teacher Training College or in University College Dublin; more important than formal learning or even the *savoir faire* that comes with adult responsibilities was the formation of an adult self capable of writing *The Barracks*. In and out of educational institutions, as student and then, from 1955 on, as a teacher, McGahern was deeply sceptical of the value of formal education, for in his own case far more important were the development of his own spiritual life and the individuating power of knowledge. While he was lucky in the circumstances he found in that small school in Carrick, and he looked back in his final decade with a sense of delight at his younger self, many earlier versions of his self-portrait suggest that adolescence was a period of intense inner conflict and desolation, with hard-won interludes of 'grace'.

One other experience of delight and grace stands out even more than the years of secondary school. The essay 'The Solitary Reader' declares that he 'had great good luck at ten or eleven'—that is, in the years immediately following his mother's death and the move to live with his father in the barracks in Cootehall: 'I was given the run of a library. I believe it changed my life and without it I would never have become a writer.' *Memoir*, which reprints much of this account written fifteen years earlier, dates the experience to 'around the same time I began life in Carrick'. This refers to the commencement of his schooling with the Presentation Brothers in Carrick-on-Shannon in September 1948, when McGahern was almost fourteen. At any rate, whatever the exact age, the two experiences are joined in his mind because in both places he discovered the intense and liberating pleasure of reading.

He first discovered 'solitary reading'—the term is actually an echo of Proust—when he began to frequent the 'nineteenth-century library' of neighbours, the Moroneys. Willie, the aging father, and Andy, his unmarried, middle-aged son, were Protestant and lived an impoverished lifestyle in an old stone house on a large farm, between the landed estates of Rockingham and Oakport, and not far from another, Woodbrook. Young John was often sent to buy apples at the Moroney farm, where he soon began to help out. The Moroneys' indifference to practical and professional matters, the personal preoccupations that took precedence, the devotion to a passion, all contributed to the charm which McGahern found in these individuals, and it was in their aura, and at Willie Moroney's suggestion, that he began to read for pleasure.

In addition to the singularly important event of providing a library throughout his adolescence, the Moroneys would supply McGahern with material for the Kirkwood stories in the 1980s, but his affection for these eccentric figures and the ambience of their lives may have had a more general early influence on him. Since they were Protestant and very poor, they were outside the sectarian and class structure of society, and as amateur philosophers and scholars they lived happily in a kind of timeless zone of decaying, ancestral security. Another way of life, a generation or two before, was embodied in the private library itself in the middle of the countryside, but McGahern reports nothing of its provenance. 'That library and those two gentle men were, to me, a pure blessing', he wrote, and so often did he credit the Moroneys with his very existence as a writer, it seems that they became symbolic figures, associated, perhaps, with Yeats and an aesthetic vision of an ideal way of life outside the stereotypes and conflicts of official Irish history and of the intimate conflicts with his father in the barracks.

'Given the run of' is the expression he used repeatedly for the adventure of exploring the Moroneys' library. It suggests the freedom he felt in being able to choose whatever he wished from the hundreds of books:

> There was Scott, Dickens, Meredith and Shakespeare, Zane Grey and Jeffrey Farnol, and many, many books about the Rocky Mountains...I didn't differentiate, I read for nothing but pleasure, the way a boy nowadays might watch endless television dramas. Every week or fortnight, for years, I'd return with five or six books in my oilcloth shopping bag and take five or six away. Nobody gave me direction or advice.[4]

In recalling the pleasure of this formative experience, he expresses surprise that his father set no limits to what he read nor enquired into it at all whereas, in general, he was censorious and prescriptive; for many years, McGahern was a secret reader of comics, something his father thoroughly disapproved of as a waste of time. (This mildly subversive situation is captured in 'Strandhill, the Sea'.) In the matter of reading books from Moroneys', however, the young McGahern appears to have entered a privileged space, set away from his father's influence and interference: 'as long as they didn't take from work or prayer I was allowed to read without hindrance'. He was in his own private world of imagination, choosing books according to his own preference or at random, yet a criterion for judgement was being formed which undoubtedly remained with him and governed his later taste. That criterion was his own pleasure: 'Pleasure is by no means an infallible, critical guide, W. H. Auden wrote; but it is the least fallible.'[5] When he wondered if he would have turned out differently had his reading been guided and structured, McGahern is really crediting the pleasure of those days as a foundation for his own very independent mind. Unhampered by any obligation to read books that had been approved of by authorities of any stripe—parents, church, or school—he became his own master and relished the freedom and power granted to him in the ritual of reading. That confident sense that he was free to make his own judgements remained for life, a necessary element, perhaps, of any writer's single-mindedness, and his likes and dislikes in literature were always fearlessly stated.

While this image of a boy in his own world may convey a sense of how he escaped from his father's aggression or began to develop a confident sense of self in adolescence, his capacity for concentration and pleasure is key to the formation of a distinctive self. 'There are no days more full in childhood than those days that were not lived at all, the days lost in a favourite book.' This often repeated sentence is an almost verbatim transcription of Proust's opening sentence in 'Ruskin and Others', and Proust's descriptions of his own mesmerized experience of reading permeates McGahern's account. It has, of course, the ring of lost time and the dream of memory giving to those days a fullness of meaning because of their link to the *moi profond*. It is in this sense that the days are 'full', although 'not lived at all': we live through our imaginations, he means, the depth of pleasure in reading becoming a measure of the depth of the self.

He tells a story to illustrate his 'complete absorption when all sense of time is lost'. So removed could he become from his physical environment that in the middle of the crowded barracks kitchen his sisters removed a shoe and placed a straw hat on his head while he continued to read unawares. He speaks of 'waking' out of a book, which suggests that the experience is a kind of hypnosis or sleep, or, perhaps, most of all, a kind of dream-state. Undoubtedly, his retrospective account of these years is shadowed by his later love of Proust's essays on reading, yet in the depths of north County Roscommon, in the 1940s, a young man underwent a transformation that enabled him, in the aftermath of his mother's death and in the surroundings of his father's volatility and violence, to experience 'a strange and complete kind of happiness'. Later, he associated this happiness with writing, although it came only in rare moments, yet it is not difficult to imagine that the transition from reading to the 'secret vocation' of writing was given purpose and energy by such 'timeless' episodes. These somewhat mystical experiences are the foundation of his later, again Proustian, view that the writer and the reader are identical when they become capable of accessing the timeless, hidden self, in which a spiritual life has its origin.

While he had the 'free run' of the Moroneys' library and borrowed books for reading at home and in the rowboat which he would take out on Oakport Lake, the routine work and accomplishments of school added other dimensions to the formation of his imagination. Realizing that in those years of the 1940s secondary education was available only to 'the rich or the academically bright', McGahern considered it a further example of his good luck that in the summer of 1948, when he was thirteen years old, the Presentation Brothers opened the school in Carrick. He was, of course, one of the 'academically bright' and won a half-scholarship. A year earlier, his father had threatened to withdraw him from school and send him to work as an accounts clerk, and he had to be persuaded of the merits of further education for his son. Now, in September 1948, John–or Seán, as he was then universally known[6]—began to cycle each morning 8 miles from Cootehall to Carrick and back each evening, 16 miles each day, yet he appears to have considered it no hardship, compared to the manual labour he was obliged to do for his father's small businesses: saving turf on the bog or picking potatoes on a rented field, the work of spring and autumn, which his father put ahead of schoolwork. His intellectual capacity was recognized—'at worst it appeals to one's vanity'—and he remembered the brilliance of his teachers, one in particular, Brother Placid. The teachers and the camaraderie of his fellow-students as they played handball or roamed the town opened another social world to the young McGahern. Through the education he received there, he broke free from his father's dark world, and the joy of imaginative and intellectual liberation was reinforced.

While his feeling about the whole experience at Carrick is rapturous, his English teacher and the literature curriculum appear to have struck a special nerve. Frank Mannion was an inspiring figure who 'had a feeling for language'. 'He gave us an essay to write every week. I suppose that was my first publication. It was part of the work that I probably enjoyed most. Mannion would read out good sentences and sometimes he might read out a whole essay. He would also read out bad sentences.'[7] He lent his own books to his students and 'would talk to me about them inside and outside school hours'. The texts McGahern studied and memorized were of the traditional canon: '*Macbeth, Henry IV*, Wordsworth's "[The] Prelude", "Tintern Abbey", Tennyson's "In Memoriam", "The Ode to Virgil"—"Thou that singest wheat and woodland/tilth and vineyard, hive and horse and herd"'. Undoubtedly, such lines appealed to him, as he cycled through 'wheat and woodland', but the poetry of memory, of Wordsworth, must have had a lasting impact, and indeed he became a writer of memory, not only in his own fiction but also in his ability to recall and recite favourite lines and passages. This is true not only of passages learned at this time, but later, as he discovered the pleasure of Yeats, Auden, and Proust, certain lines and sentences were added to his store of literary quotations which remained a vital part of his life and would often turn up in conversation. Clearly part of the lasting pleasure of cycling to Carrick is captured here: 'I used to chant them aloud when I cycled alone in and out to school on those empty roads. Sometimes I chanted the Ordinary of the Mass, since I now knew the words by heart and they were beginning to take on meaning through Caesar and Virgil and Cicero and Horace.'[8] Above and beyond memorization for his classes, the pleasure of chanting, poetry or Latin deepened his pleasure in the literature itself, and memory was put to use in that special way to enlarge his imaginative perception. A further kind of private empowerment is associated with this ritual of chanting as he cycled through the largely unpopulated landscape. He made the classics of English and Latin his own.

The development of a memory for literature became a part of him that had vital significance. 'What is good writing but memorable speech?' McGahern asked, in talking about the importance of teaching young children to memorize poems the teacher liked, and he stressed the importance of the teacher developing an individual feeling for poetry. He goes on to mention lyric poems he taught successfully himself, and his choice surely reflects what he had loved and memorized earlier: 'Some of Shakespeare's, like "Under the Greenwood Tree"; some of Hardy's. "Ariel's Song" from *The Tempest*; some of the early Yeats. "Though You Are in your Shining Days".' This line, from Yeats's poem 'The Lover Pleads with his Friend for Old Friends', also comes into the mind of the teacher/mother in *The Leavetaking*, and this 'secret' lover of poetry explains something that must surely represent McGahern's own view: 'What gives me most pleasure still from my own schooling are the poems I learned by heart then; constantly I find them passing through my mind, not unlike old friends or stray strands of music.'[9] This short episode in the novel, focused on the decision facing the young teacher to continue with her engagement to the sergeant or to break it and become a nun, seems to include a characterization of the mother which is actually autobiographical: the choice between being a priest or a poet/teacher was the one actually facing McGahern himself as he neared the end of secondary school. This is not the place to explore the ideas of the teacher/mother on poetry, mostly derived from Yeats, but her appreciation of 'some magical twist, which I believe is the infusion of the poetical personality into the words'[10] is surely apropos at this point. The pleasure, the chanting, the memorization are all intimately related to this discovery of 'poetical personality' in language and to the appreciation of something mysterious, akin to magic, that could become available to the writer.

The fears and dreams of young Mahoney in *The Dark* draw on what was certainly part of McGahern's experience at Carrick, and many circumstantial details in the novel are repeated in interviews McGahern gave and in *Memoir*. There are two versions of his secondary schooling. *The Dark* dramatizes very intimately the way the boy felt, trapped in his father's world, and trapped too in a competitive examination system, the outcome of which would determine his future. The reader shares the boy's existential struggle to manage his feelings as he faces an unknown future, but when McGahern recalled his own schooldays, he knew the outcome and the future. He speaks of this period as a time of liberation from his father's world and from his childhood, but it would only be his own later success that would allow him to read his past definitively in this light.

That liberation came to him through Shakespeare and the other classic texts he studied. The solitary pleasure of reading books from the Moroneys' library certainly stayed with him, and he often spoke of it as the definitive experience that made him a writer, but it is also worth considering what he may have absorbed from those years studying English. *The Dark* suggests that what is learned for exams is quickly forgotten:

> I gathered and put away the books that night. The nights of slavery, cramming the mind for the exam, most of it useless rubbish, and already being forgotten. The most that was left was some of the Latin lyrics, their strange grace; *Macbeth*; some poems; and the delight of solving the maths problems, putting order on their enclosed world, proving that numbers real and imaginary had relationships with each other.[11]

The pleasure of abstract reasoning, of an 'enclosed world', of finding relationships between the real and the imaginary suggests that he might have become a mathematician, although his account seems to set little difference between mathematics and writing a poem, except perhaps for the 'grace' of the final text. The narrator seems to say that little is worth remembering, and memorizing passages from Shakespeare seems to fit that formula, and yet this is highly unlikely. Apart from the training of the memory, and the storing of what is memorized, how was McGahern's literary sensibility influenced by the poems and the plays, the classic texts that he studied and memorized?

It is impossible to trace such formative influences, or to answer a question such as why did he not become a poet, if poetry was central to the curriculum. In spite of this, certain speculations may serve. For instance, young Mahoney's last evening before the exams begin is almost unbearable: ' "Yes, tomorrow", I nodded. "Tomorrow and tomorrow and tomorrow", started to beat to the mind out of *Macbeth*.'[12] He had to learn off the passage, and he will remember its echo, but apart from the dramatic power of character and action in that play, the unforgettable Macbeth and Lady Macbeth or the three witches, the madness and fierce ambition, the suspense, all the ingredients of the drama, these words are not simply a worn tagline, for—like so many lines from Shakespeare which have entered common speech—they carry a depth of resonance. Is it too much to believe that the whole passage entered McGahern's memory, its eloquence, its poetry, and its existential meaning:

> Tomorrow, and tomorrow, and tomorrow
> Creeps in this petty pace from day to day,
> To the last syllable of recorded time;
> And all our yesterdays have lighted fools
> The way to dusty death. Out, out, brief candle!
> Life's but a walking shadow, a poor player,
> That struts and frets his hour upon the stage,
> And then is heard no more; it is a tale
> Told by an idiot, full of sound and fury,
> Signifying nothing.

Macbeth, V.5.19–28

Young Mahoney's fearful sensibility, and that of his anguished father—' "This is my life, and this kitchen in the townland of Cloone is my stage, and I am playing my life out here on", and he stood, the eyes wild, as if grappling for his lines'[13]—appear to reflect something of these sentiments; he has not simply memorized a speech for exam purposes. The urgent questioning of meaning and purpose that all Shakespeare's tragedies dramatize is surely reflected in his father's life and in his own humble life.

And so, when we know that McGahern studied *Henry IV*, it is hard to believe that he was not moved to absorb into himself such lines as: 'But thought's the slave of life, and life time's fool, / And time, that takes survey of all the world, / Must have a stop' (*Henry IV, Part One*, V.4.80–2). Or that the sonnet beginning 'Like as the waves make towards the pebbled shore, / So do our minutes hasten to their end' did not colour and bring to articulation a sensibility that was already preoccupied with such sentiments. The memorable poetry of Shakespeare's vision may have stayed with McGahern, more vivid even than the great characters of the tragedies, the affairs of state of the history plays, the sense of fate and tragic flaws that bring the house down. Woven into *The Barracks* is a second-hand reference to Falstaff, used to characterize one of the guards: 'Who are they to say that we shall have no more cakes and ale?' It is a sentiment as close to McGahern's adult outlook as the other more lugubrious one, but the point is similar: he had a repertoire of Shakespearean allusions to draw on, and it is likely that they became part of him at this time.[14] Although he may not have studied *Hamlet* or *King Lear* for his Leaving Certificate curriculum, they do appear on his third-level curricula, and the great soliloquies of those plays are echoed in his fiction. Indeed, it is the status of interior monologue as a technique for dramatizing character that suggests what he really took from Shakespeare. His characters, much like Hamlet, ask themselves 'To be or not to be' and the fiction represents the struggle to find answers to that conundrum. Rather than being novels and stories grounded in plot or action, they are fictions of consciousness, the drama being, like drama in Shakespeare, a poetic expansion of the felt inner life of the characters.

Over and over in interviews, McGahern referred to fiction as the *dramatization* of the inner life, and the success or failure of writing depended on the depth and clarity of that revelation. Interior monologue on a large scale is central to McGahern's own vision, but it is also worth considering that his love of the theatre during his years in Dublin may reflect an early desire to use the theatre as his literary medium. At many times during his career, he tried his hand at plays for radio, adapted some of his own stories, and, in 1972, his version of Tolstoy's *The Power of Darkness* was broadcast on BBC radio. He had also prepared a stage version of Tolstoy's play at this time, and a revision of this went on at the Abbey Theatre in 1991, but he continued to rework it to the end of his life, as if for more than thirty years he had struggled to get this one play right. But in many ways his fiction incorporates important elements of poetic drama. If he took an intense pleasure from the novels he borrowed from the Moroneys and from his English teacher, his literary training in poetry and drama ensured that they—perhaps more than plot or character—would be the foundation of his fictional method.

'In the beginning was my mother', he wrote in *Memoir*, in echo of the biblical 'In the beginning was the Word, and the Word was with God and the Word was God.' Mother, Word, and God. It is surely interesting that the mother/teacher in *The Leavetaking* is dramatized as someone who might have been a nun, whose love of poetry is paramount, is, in fact, a private faith: 'It can be felt, but not known, as we can never know our own life or another's in the great mystery of life.'[15] Her poems and prayers are one, her literature equal to her gospel. She is an autobiographical image, of course, expressing ideas and referring to Yeats in ways that we associate with the author of the novel. At the same time, the mother/teacher is imagined as an ideal reader who brings to her love of poetry a profound faith in its power to communicate a sense of metaphysical reality, 'the great mystery'. McGahern would refer to his first novel, *The Barracks*, as 'a religious poem', and even *The Dark*, so notoriously banned on the instigation of the Catholic Archbishop of Dublin, he described as 'a religious work if it's anything at all'.[16] Long after he was no longer a believer, and long after his mother's death, he still thought of writing in relation to her image, and, whatever he might mean by 're-ligious' in literary terms, it is clear that one way of thinking about his identity as a writer is to consider the lasting place in his imagination of his mother's pious faith, her intuitive sense of the 'great mystery'.

The world-view and practices of Catholicism pervaded McGahern's familial and communal life, a form of inherited know-ledge available to him in adolescence, just as much as the landscape of the Shannon region and the people he observed there were givens. In her life and in her death, Susan McGahern provided her son with an image of trust in a universal and transcending know-ledge, and his participation in church rituals and ceremonies were for him, he repeated many times, a source of sensual pleasure and delight. 'The church dominated the little village', he wrote, 'an ex-tension of the house and the barracks, but with different laws and a higher authority, and it opened outwards...The church ceremonies always gave me pleasure, and I miss them even now. In an impoverished time they were my first introduction to an indoor beauty, of luxury and ornament, ceremony and sacrament and mystery.'[17] He refers to a young visiting priest whose sermons introduced him to the idea that 'reflection on the mystery of life was itself a form of prayer', and this may be the sense in which *The Barracks* and *The Dark* are religious in a more fundamental way than the 'empty formulas' of common worship. He went on to say that:

> before the printed word, the churches were the Bibles of the poor, and the Church was my first book. The story of Christ as I followed it through these ceremonies gave meaning and depth to both the year and our lives. The way was travelled not only in suffering but in ecstasy. I was introduced to all I have come to know of prayer and sacrament, ceremony and mystery, grace and ornament and the equality of all women and men underneath the sun of heaven.[18]

He wrote as if the rituals and ceremonies, and the cosmic knowledge associated with them, remained all his life as an inheritance, an orientation that underlay all later forms of knowledge, but this conviction is associated primarily with his mother's faith and his memories of her.

One of the most powerful and affecting scenes in McGahern's work is the recreation of the days of his mother's death and funeral. The public rituals follow the Catholic observances so that everyone moves within a well-known structure for mourning. This begins as soon as her death is announced in the barracks. Frank McGahern leads his family in a recitation of the rosary for the repose of the soul of Susan McGahern. The long public prayer in which everyone participates, reciting in turn the five decades of ten Hail Marys, the responses, and the litanies, was a daily event in the McGahern family, as in most Irish Catholic families at the time. The family, the community, the country, and the whole world, according to the statements of the One, Holy, Catholic and Apostolic Church, were given a means to bear bereavement and suffering, to find hope and justice in an afterlife. But if this communal prayer provides the father with a ritual that structures his feeling, the children's grief cannot be contained by it. So intense is the boy's reaction that it follows a different path, from the moment he experiences 'the unreal memory that yesterday she died'.[19] His memory runs over the years of his life with her, all those images of childhood recalled with ease, his grief embedding them deeper in him, so that when he writes *The Leavetaking* thirty years later and *Memoir* sixty years later, they reappear on the page in arresting detail and are the substance of his childhood with his mother.

But these recollections of days actually spent with her are followed the next day by a concentrated and panic-stricken imagining of the two stages of the funeral service, which the young boy was not allowed to attend. First he imagines her body being removed from the deathbed, placed in a coffin, and the lid closed; then the carrying of the coffin to the hearse, the journey to the church, and the prayers. Next day, the day of her burial, he takes the kitchen clock at the hour of her funeral mass, and, hidden in the laurels, lives the minutes by imagining step by step what is happening in Aughawillan church. He can cope with his grief only by imagining the scene, by participating in it, although he is not there. The temporal gap between the boy of nine and the writer many decades later is blurred; the boy holding the clock is the writer making time stand still. Imagining of such intense vividness is as real as actually living, perhaps, indeed, more real than living itself for space and time are abolished in this hour when the boy/artist transports himself to his mother's graveside. The aura of a spiritual reality is as much rooted in his own mind as in the rituals and myths of the Church. His mother is an image of another order of reality, which is both mortal and immortal, subjective and objective. She exists in a reality which is at once religious and imaginative.

McGahern's recreation of his lost mother became a private ritual in the years following her death, and the images that are recalled and the ways in which the culture structured his memories for him gave him his earliest material for fiction, but it is surely the power of memory itself and its capacity to recover lost knowledge involuntarily that is most fundamental to his work. It is for this reason that he found in Proust's great novel, his essays, and his letters a supreme value in recreating one's own earlier experience.

When John McGahern reflected on his emergence as a writer, he often credited luck and accident as the key conditions, including the 'good luck' of having an offer from Faber and Faber in March 1961 to publish *The Barracks*, at this stage only just begun. In his final written statement, he declared 'The god of life is accident', and went on to say: 'Fiction has to be true to a central idea or vision of life.'[20] In his own case, certainly, and in the vision of life embodied in his fiction, it is easy to see the central place occupied by the random events of life—his mother's illness and death, in particular—but equally central are the predictable forces of nature and culture: time passing, human instincts, the imprints of history. In that statement, written as a Preface to his final selection of his stories, he admits to uncertainty and improvisation in the way fiction emerges according to its own lights, but he also insists that it must be 'true to a central idea' and insofar as that is so, fiction is shaped by clear thinking. The parts played by talent and poetic sensibility are, obviously, unfathomable—the province of the 'god of accident'—but the part played by intelligence in shaping fiction around a central idea may be traced. There is a place for knowledge and for 'training' in the clarification of poetic 'vision' and in the critical discriminations of literary traditions.

In the private pleasure of unrestricted reading, and the memorization and chanting of poetry, he was apart from his five sisters and from everyone in the barracks home. He would withdraw to the Boyle river behind the house and drift out into the lake to read in the boat, or he would simply become absorbed in the midst of things. Over the years, the nature of his reading changed 'to a different order of pleasure that was both recognition and discovery and sometimes a pure unfathomable joy'. This is how he described the change in *Memoir*, but a decade earlier he had written: 'this change is linked with our growing consciousness, consciousness that we will not live forever and that all human life is in the same fix. We have to discard all the tenets we have been told until we have succeeded in thinking them out for ourselves.'[21] This increasing knowledge of a distinct selfhood appears to reflect a stage of questioning in adolescence, although when McGahern speaks of discarding received understanding or 'tenets' (a word that appears to be shorthand for religious beliefs), he does not introduce any sense of intellectual or emotional crisis. Rather, this stage of 'recognition and discovery' is linked to joy, as if the imaginative pleasure of reading and intellectual enlargement are continuous, as if for him the 'adventure' of learning and knowledge expanded awareness in a way that he welcomed and was not disruptive or alienating in its erosion of given truths.

Years earlier, he had spoken of this stage in a slightly different way. 'From being marvellous stories, like movies, and marvellous songs, which words always are for me, you suddenly realize that these things are about your own life. Literature changes from being books in a library to something that concerns you. In fact, it loses some of its exoticism. That's when it becomes a more exciting activity, a moral activity.' Associating this change primarily with Yeats, he goes on to explain: 'I do think that the pleasure that words give is the comfort of generality. Each person lives in his own isolation and out of that the particular is given the grace of ceremony, is given the grace of the general.'[22] 'Grace, actual grace' was the word he used to describe what he was fortunate to receive in his school in Carrick-on-Shannon, and here that word appears to be explained: 'the grace of the general'. In other words, it seems that solitary reading did not feel to him an isolating activity; rather, he found through it that his own isolated experience could be generalized; that, in reading, he could discover others who understood and sympathized and explained his own experience to him, or at least helped him to see that underlying the personal was the communal, which was, perhaps, the common experience known as human nature.

The 'moral activity' of reading in this new stage was, then, the discovery that reading and thinking affirmed a knowledge that one was not alone even in one's most isolated moments. Literature offered a 'ceremony' that linked the individual to the common experience of humanity at large. And so, the obvious next step was to discover through reading how one might become a writer who could share this moral experience, as well as a liberating joy, with others:

> We begin to come on certain books that act like mirrors. What they reflect is something dangerously close to our own life and the society in which we live. A new, painful excitement enters the way we read. We search out these books, and these books only, the books that act

as mirrors. The quality of the writing becomes more important than the quality of the material out of which the pattern or story is shaped.[23]

As often, in McGahern's allusions to his own evolution and practice as an artist, the words of Proust shadow his language—as here, 'books that act as mirrors'—but the young man had experienced such an awakening already in Shakespeare and Yeats before he came upon Proust. The searching-out of those special books, learning how to recognize the unique quality of writing, the particular style in which personal value lay for him, became central to John McGahern's apprenticeship in the Dublin years.

2

The Vocation

In September 1953, aged eighteen, McGahern left home in the barracks at Cootehall and entered St Patrick's Training College in Dublin. He had some doubts about his decision to answer the 'call to training' as a primary schoolteacher, for even though the records show he registered at St Pat's on 19 September, the records of University College Galway show that he also registered there, in the Faculty of Agricultural Science, on 7 October.[1] Two weeks later, he withdrew from Galway, and so he settled in to the training programme at St Pat's which would last for the next two years. 'I'd never have been a teacher, I see clearly, except for my mother', Patrick Moran in *The Leavetaking* reflects, and he is sure that his mother's influence was a shadow from which he must free himself. As McGahern's own deathbed promise to his mother that he would become a priest became less binding, he turned to teaching: 'The guilt I felt at turning my back halfheartedly—on the death in life that was the priest's choice and on that dear promise to say Mass—I was able to partially resolve by telling myself that teaching was my mother's profession and was sometimes called the second priesthood.'[2] This suggests that in the 'second priesthood' he is preserving a continuity that might otherwise be betrayed. The characterization of the teacher/mother in *The Leavetaking* as a lover of poetry is a clear indication that priest, teacher, and writer are all devoted to nurturing the spiritual life, yet the discovery of individual freedom is dramatized as a liberation into a new life beyond inherited roles and feelings.

Memoir makes clear the autobiographical basis of this bond to the mother. Yet, even if the high-minded image of his mother was a semi-conscious reason why the decision to become a teacher prevailed, McGahern had another secret reason for answering the 'call to training'. 'The real reason I was going I told no one. The teaching hours were short. There were long holidays. I wouldn't have to think about money. These were all the means I needed to follow my dream.' That dream was, of course, to become a writer, the plan that came to him during his solitary hours reading on the river. 'Over many days and months, gradually, a fantastical idea formed. Why take on any single life—a priest, a soldier, teacher, doctor, airman—if a writer could create all these people far more vividly. In that one life of the mind, the writer could live many lives and all of life.'[3] Presenting the decision in this way reinforces the idea that the single-minded young man of eighteen was clear in his purposes, that his 'secret vocation' defined him from this point on. While the dream of being born again 'as the god of a small, vivid world' is a 'fantastical idea' in the mind of the young man on the Boyle river in 1953, it is equally fantastical that he would have the prescience to know that a salary, short working hours, and long holidays would be the means to the end. The solemnity of this claim in *Memoir* is downplayed: 'I had not even the vaguest idea of how books came into being, but the dream took hold, and held...I must have had some sense of how outrageous and laughable this would appear to the world, because I told no one, but it did serve its first purpose—it set me free.' In this retrospective recreation, the revelation that came to him is a kind of religious experience, a vision of coming to know the essence of things—'all of life'—rather than merely the professional roles and circumstances.

Embedded in the brief description of this time are echoes from McGahern's later reading, so that it is possible to see this as an interpretation of his conversion to the artistic life, rather than a report on what the young man actually thought or knew. The sentence 'In that one life of the mind, the writer could live many lives and all of life', for instance, comes close to repeating the words in which he expressed his admiration for Joyce and *Dubliners*. 'Joyce does not judge. His characters live within the human constraints in space and time and within their own city...In their richness and truth [they] are representations of particular lives—and all of life.'[4] It would be some years before McGahern would read Joyce or recognize in him a fellow 'clerk' working in a classical tradition, and admire *Dubliners* and 'the great passages of *Ulysses*' in which he believed Joyce remains faithful to 'his first characters, his original material'. It would also be some years before he would read Flaubert's letters and find there the origin of Joyce's remark (as McGahern reports it): 'The author is like God in nature, present everywhere but nowhere visible.' Such phrases are clearly in the mind of the author of *Memoir*, however, so that, in spite of his stated wish to distance himself from *A Portrait of the Artist as a Young Man*, the ghostly presence of Stephen Dedalus, who decided not to become a priest and to seek an absolute freedom 'in silence exile and cunning', haunts these words.

The author of *Memoir* seems to claim a confidence and clear-sightedness for his younger self which were the equal of the Jesuit-trained Joyce, something that stands out in contrast to the characterization of young Mahoney in *The Dark*, at sea in the university milieu. That milieu was precisely where Dedalus thrived, displaying his learning on all sides. McGahern did contrast elsewhere his own schooling with the metropolitan literary education Joyce received, but in *Memoir* the boy from the country in his tar-bottomed boat will not be characterized as timid or backward or at the mercy of events. In spite of disclaimers of naiveté, McGahern wants to honour his young self: the decision to be a teacher was as cunning a move as any made by Joyce, he seems to say. He would not leave Ireland to achieve his dream; he would be an inner exile.

It may be that the 'secret vocation' that led McGahern to choose to be a teacher was still vague in his mind, yet it was in the very real circumstances of the teacher training college that it became clearer. In the summer of 1953, he was one of an elite group of school-leavers with the highest academic standing. All the expenses of the training college were covered, tuition and accommodation, and also, unlike what many university faculties offered, the training was a professional one which would certainly lead on to a teaching post. At St Patrick's, most of the students were from the country, and many would return to teach in rural Ireland. The role of teacher was viewed as an important one in country parishes. It was a privileged position, but, since the management of national schools was exclusively in the hands of parish priests, it came with the high price of conformity and orthodoxy. And conformity and orthodoxy were inculcated in St Patrick's at the expense of intellectual or personal development.

McGahern's experience at the training college was evidently a very different kind of education from what he had expected to receive in a third-level city institution. While the teaching practice he received prepared him for work in the classroom, the intellectual and cultural milieu, and especially the institutional structures of St Pat's, gave him much food for thought regarding the place of the teacher in Irish society and indeed the nature of that society. His comments suggest that he underwent a profound disillusionment, an awakening to a recognition that the life of the mind was valued much less than the perpetuation of authoritarian control; to a recognition that, in fact, the teachers were being trained to be 'non-commissioned officers' in the Church's unrelenting battle to maintain absolute control over the behaviour of individuals and over public discourse. It is probably not an exaggeration to say that in his first year in St Pat's the boy from the country received a vivid introduction to the nature of a theocracy. What had been implicit in his early years now became visible to him: the Church was the agent of pervasive social control, with 'unquestioned power' in the 'infant' state. 'It was the dominating force in my whole upbringing and education and early working life',[5] although his bemused comments about Canon Glynn in Cootehall suggest that he was not conscious of the Church as a 'dominating force' there. The contrast he draws between his secondary education with the enlightened Presentation Brothers in Carrick and the training College regime, and later the Christian Brothers' school in Drogheda where he worked, suggest that it was when he left the countryside that he recognized the Church as a formidably repressive and punitive national institution. It was at this time, perhaps, that he began to associate his father's sadistic and self-righteous behaviour with this authoritarian, punitive organization.

Although McGahern's drift away from the Catholic faith may have been far advanced by this stage, it is likely that in observing the way the institution of St Pat's worked he recognized that the Church for the most part had little to do with the life of the mind or of the spirit. He became a dissenter from now to the end of his time as a teacher in 1965, when he was fired. That dissent was kept private from most people—his father was an exception, *Memoir* reveals—and became embodied in the fiction he worked on in his first decade. In later years, he would spell out his profound opposition to this system of coercion, 'created at the expense of intelligence, insight and judgement', and the distinction he would later insist on between morals and the spiritual life almost certainly has its foundation here.

Unlike many of his colleagues who had been boarders at diocesan colleges, McGahern was unused to a regime governed by coercion. 'Each college day began with morning Mass and ended with evening Devotions in the chapel…Not to attend daily Mass or evening Devotions was to invite certain expulsion.'[6] Mealtimes were barbaric, with those skilled in the boarding-house reach leaving little food for those not so quick. 'You'd starve if you had any manners. I saw the Dean beat up a student in full view of the refectory because he had complained too vociferously that he hadn't got his boiled egg.'[7] That student is identified as his close friend Éanna Ó hEither, an Irish-speaker from the Aran Islands who played a decisive role in freeing McGahern from the insularity of the institution. Ó hEither was exceptional, because the pettiness of those who enforced authority was mirrored by many of the boys who were conformist and pious. 'Childishness was nurtured and encouraged to last a whole life long', McGahern concludes. Kinds of 'half-barbaric' behaviour, other than at mealtimes, exerted the coercive power of peer pressure and ridicule. In fact, this threat and the routines that controlled social life and enforced a devotional regime ensured that the primary focus was on the suitability of the individual for the life of conformity ahead. 'What was under scrutiny at all times was our "character", not in the true sense of the word, but in the sense that we would be religious in observance, obedient and conventional, cogs in an organizational wheel.' Docility was the first virtue. The threat of expulsion was, of course, the whip of an authority which could cut off a whole life's promise, for, after expulsion, the boys knew 'there was nothing but the emigrant boat'. It is obvious in such comments that McGahern found the system dehumanizing and contemptuous of the individual person. His anger is palpable forty years later, an anger that certainly made its way into an early story such as 'The Recruiting Officer'.

The ambience was actually, in McGahern's view, deliberately anti-intellectual. In his recollections, he does not mention a single admirable teacher; instead, he recalls the crazed disciplinary gestures of the Dean of Studies, 'the Bat' (Fr. Johnston). 'All the societies in the college were religious. There wasn't a literary or historical or philosophical or, even more surprising still, a Gaelic society.' A few students tried to set up an intellectual society, 'four or five people who actually discussed Wilde and behaved as one would expect third-level students to do. They were nicknamed "*Oideachas Eireann*" and they were hounded.' Well trained in the barracks, he kept his head down in such circumstances: 'I was too careful or fearful to belong to it... I was more interested in survival... I knew that it would get me into trouble.'[8] In fact, in another context, he says somewhat bitterly that his was 'a silent generation'. It was a censored generation, for the silence was enforced in many ways, including the censorship of reading and ideas; McGahern appears to have become aware of this for the first time in St Pat's for he later referred to 'the powerful unofficial censorship' which pervaded the institution and the rural society: 'There was something considered wrong and dangerous and idle about reading books. The only purpose for reading books was to pass exams... This fellow would prowl up and down the study hall, and if you were reading Eliot or some book that wasn't on the course, you could actually get biffed at the back of your ears.' This is a personal experience, for he did discover T. S. Eliot for the first time then, from Éanna Ó hEither, and other modern writers from students who were 'hounded'. In retrospect, it is clear that McGahern feels he has ground to make up for a lack of courage—'Ambrose Bierce's definition of a coward is one who in an emergency thinks with his heels'—and one cannot help thinking that in his later defiance of conventional restraints in *The Dark* or *The Pornographer*, aesthetic intentions may be coloured by a moral outrage, even a salving of his own conscience for earlier silence. While he remarked later that the official censorship did not bother serious readers, who could find the banned books anyhow, it is this pervasive 'unofficial censorship' that had the more profound effect in the society as a whole.

At St Pat's McGahern was an adept conformist and a secret subversive. The repressive regime maintained by the priests and staff did not repress him. Indeed, it became a place for acute observation of the rules of the game and a training ground in public role-playing. It may well have sharpened his skills at performance and concealment, may have heightened his awareness of the gap between the secret life of private feeling and thought and the public mask required for social interactions.

In his final decades, he would charm audiences with a polished public presence (although not without stage nerves), but he probably learned at a young age how to engage and divert an audience. Before using this talent in the classroom, he had used it in St Pat's. The ability to deflect attention from personal vulnerability into song, story, or joke is a common talent in Irish culture, and whether it is seen as a historical inheritance developed for alleviating poverty and distress, or as another form of repression, it is certain that McGahern knew well how to use it when he needed to. A chapter in *The Dark* reveals the children gaining release from the father's oppression through laughter and mockery of him, and, indeed, there is a suggestion there that the father can be mocked because of his own theatricality. In St Pat's, McGahern recognized that his talent could be a useful tool for gaining control in a diverting way. It was a clear sign of intelligence, but it also suggests that his interest in theatre grew out of an innate interest in the power of the public performance.

There is reason to believe that, as a young man, he was at ease in public and the evidence comes from his own anecdotes and of others who knew him. Stories told by a classmate convey an image of a confident joker, alert to opportunities to go one better than his teachers by appealing to his fellow-students.[9] In English class, he helped out this classmate by stage-managing a short comic drama to illustrate the concept of racial stereotyping—the 'stage Irishman'— and, on another occasion, hammed it up when asked what the word for moon in different languages suggested. Although *Memoir* implies that he made little effort to work at his various subjects—'you were neither more nor less a national teacher whether you got 90 or 40'—it is clear that his brilliance was recognized, in English, at any rate, and, out of the school, he appears to have had a quick wit and to have enjoyed camaraderie and fun. In fact, in later years, he cultivated this comic ease, in marked contrast to the intense artistic persona of his middle years.

He was sensitive to the performative aspects of language, to personality and voice. A skit he wrote at St Pat's was incorporated thirty years later into his only television drama, *The Rockingham Shoot*, which is set in a national school. A talent for entertaining others, much in evidence in later years in his relaxed conversational moments, emerged early, and this suggests why he will take a keen interest in the theatre; in a more tragic-comic mode, it will be an ingredient of his fiction, in dialogue and in dramatic scenes. The skill in performance will be useful in his career as a teacher, but it is tempting to think that he learned something of the power of performance from his own father; *Memoir* gives considerable weight to the word of a cousin who suggested that the father's enigmatic character could be understood: he was an actor. The power and control that the father wielded in the family and in the community came partly from how he set up dramatic scenes; the novelist may have started out as his understudy. McGahern seems to be aware of this, for so many scenes in the novels and stories portray the father in this way—the long silence punctuated by an abrupt remark, the build-up of tension, the controlling gestures. The letters of the father reprinted in *Memoir* reveal a commanding power of language, but in this he met his match. One of the truly arresting remarks comes when McGahern explains that, while still a student, he wrote replies for his sister Rosaleen to the father's terrorizing rants. He enjoyed the job of assuming his sister's voice to control the father: 'the masks set me free'. That performative power eventually became part of his persona as a writer.

Early in his first year in St Pat's, McGahern discovered that the classical English literature he had known, and which Mr Mannion had taught him with such enthusiasm, was only a small part of the overall picture; that there were great writers of the modern period he had not heard of, as well as great writers in other languages. The excitement of this discovery did not come to him in the classroom. 'What education I picked up when I was [at St Pat's] was from fellow students. A brilliant classmate...Éanna Ó hEither, who was a dear friend, first put Joyce and Eliot in my hand.'[10] The independence and literary discrimination of Ó hEither, and of his older brother, Breandán, were due in part to their contact with their uncle Liam O'Flaherty, the internationally known novelist and short-story writer who had grown up on the Aran Islands. Not only did McGahern awaken, with some regret for his tardiness, to the existence of major figures of the twentieth century but he discovered that there were living authors, such as O'Flaherty, whose presence and whose work had the vital force of contemporaries. While Shakespeare, Wordsworth, and Tennyson had existed in a kind of timeless zone in school books, not much different from the timeless zone in which the books in Moroneys' library existed, the work of the moderns represented an engagement with the world in which one had to find one's own way.

Even if McGahern did not read O'Flaherty's work extensively, this cosmopolitan and local artist surely influenced the reading habits of his nephew, and it was he who introduced McGahern to Dostoevsky. Later, McGahern would say that he read everything by Dostoevsky in the training college, and he, rather than Tolstoy, Chekhov, or Turgenev, whose work McGahern would grow to love, was very likely his introduction to Russian literature and to European writing in translation.[11] This brief passion for Dostoevsky suggests that perhaps the intense depiction of moral and religious quest appealed to him and that he may have found an aspect of his disaffection mirrored in a character such as the protagonist of *Notes from the Underground*. Rather than the great novels, *Crime and Punishment* or *The Brothers Karamazov*, for instance, this novella may have drawn him into its meditation on issues that would preoccupy him until the late 1970s. In fact, this brief work introduced into European literature a type of alienated consciousness which McGahern appears to have responded to in writers as diverse as Camus, Thomas Mann, Kafka, Montherlant, and Céline in the following decades. His interest in such visceral soul-searching, anguish, and suffering is unmistakably registered in novels such as *The Dark* and *The Pornographer* and in *The Barracks* in the character of Halliday. The burden of self-consciousness, the moral degeneration, the inability to love or to experience spontaneous feeling, are elements of many characters who have cut themselves adrift from traditional beliefs and pieties and are struggling to feel or articulate a clear purpose in life.

In a small circle in St Pat's there was debate about the value of literature as an interpretation of modern life, the life beyond the artificial confines and pieties of the college. 'Books were discussed secretly and passed around, and I continued to read for pleasure, a pleasure that was subtly changing all the time from those first adventures in Moroneys' library.'[12] The conspiratorial atmosphere surrounding this initiation made it doubly attractive, the forbidden and the banned altogether more desirable as a dangerous truth. McGahern remarked on this and on the contemporary revolution in reading which became possible through the availability of Penguin paperbacks, in which many modern classics in translation were reprinted. Later he will value the second-hand bookshops, the free access to the National Library of Ireland, where he became a regular reader, and the literary bookshops such as the Eblana on Grafton Street where current literary magazines could be perused. Soon the city opened to him as a place where the free exchange of ideas and the sharing of intensified pleasures in reading might be possible.

This impassioned discovery of modern art, and the strength he drew from it, was not restricted to books, for he also began to go out into the city on Wednesday and Saturday afternoons and on Sunday—to dancehalls and matches at Croke Park with friends, certainly, but also to the Gate Theatre and to the cinema. The private and solitary experience of reading, intensified by friendship in St Pat's, opened out to the public culture of the city. It has often been said that the 1950s were an oppressively obscurantist period in Irish life, and to an extent McGahern argued that this was indeed the case, yet what he was able to find in Dublin was entirely liberating. 'The pleasure that found its first expression in the books of Moroneys' library', he wrote, 'was becoming wider and more various even as it deepened.'[13] This pleasure and passion, which he credits with giving him his life's vocation, are here associated with the next stage of his awakening to art, and however casual the style of the sentence, it implies that what he encountered in Dublin theatres and art cinemas was no less important.

These first visits to the Gate Theatre certainly moved him further away from conventional paths into the vibrant cultural life of the city. It is noteworthy that he attended the Gate, rather than the Abbey Theatre, and it was here that he began his education in European drama. He remembered attending performances of plays by Pirandello, Chekhov, Lorca, Beckett, Tennessee Williams, O'Casey, and recalled with affection Eugene O'Neill's *Long Day's*

Journey into Night at the end of the decade. Throughout the 1950s, he continued to attend 'pocket theatres in Georgian basements' (he is thinking primarily of the Pike, where he saw the first production of *Waiting for Godot* in early 1956 before it transferred to the Gate) and the Globe Theatre productions in the Gas Company Theatre in Dun Laoghaire.

The Gate put on Pirandello's *Henry IV* in April 1955, and this may have been McGahern's introduction to the Sicilian author for whom he developed a considerable affection. Pirandello had been recognized as a major force in European theatre from the success of *Six Characters in Search of an Author* in the 1920s, and many of his successors in experimental drama, such as Anouilh and Giradoux, were often produced in Dublin in the 1950s. Much later, McGahern will recall lines of the father character: 'But don't you see the whole trouble lies here in words, words…We think we understand each other, but we never really do.'[14] And his reference to Pirandello's story 'The Rivers of Lapland' suggests that he was drawn to the subversion of realism, to the drama of the inner world, of consciousness, memory, and dreams, indeed to madness itself as a subject of Pirandello's work. It may be that the anguish of a character like Halliday in *The Barracks*, counterpointing the agony of Elizabeth Reegan, may owe something to this, for Halliday's jokes about 'The Human Drama of Suffering' which doctors and nurses witness in hospitals are ironic; if Halliday imagines that the natural genre for such a vision of life is tragedy, his own life seems to move beyond catharsis into a form of madness and self-destruction.

Undoubtedly a central issue for McGahern was the nature of tragedy itself, for a central part of his work is a passionate effort to envision suffering and anguish and to find a redemptive art for such experience. Whether it was Pirandello's absurdist modernism, or that of Beckett, the tragi-comedy of O'Casey, the classical tragedy of O'Neill, or the bedrock work of Shakespeare, McGahern's attraction to these plays was an important part of the growth of his sensibility and his imagination in these years. It seems that he went beyond the attendance at productions to consider the theory of tragedy and comedy, as his references to Bergson's philosophical essay *On Laughter* confirm, but it is unlikely that his interest was confined to this one philosopher of the tragic.

While his attraction to the theatre had certain demonstrable influences on his work, his early love of the cinema has a less tangible influence. Certainly, he brought girls on dates to some of the blockbuster films that ran for weeks in the palatial cinemas along O'Connell Street—he referred to seeing Gielgud and Brando in *Julius Caesar* at the Metropole; this was in February–March 1954, and Orson Welles' *Othello* had an equally long run two years later. But he furthered his own mission in the small art-house cinemas that opened from 1953 on. The first and the most well known was the Astor, a tiny cinema close to O'Connell Bridge which specialized in European cinema, especially French and Italian. McGahern remembered seeing *Monsieur Hulot's Holiday*, which played there for ten weeks in 1954–5, and he probably saw *Les Règles du Jeu, Casque d'Or*, and *Les Enfants du Paradis* in the Astor. In fact, in this cinema, he was exposed to a rich harvest of the best of current and classic European films, including the early films of Bergman, work by De Sica and Renoir, Bresson and René Clair, Fellini, Truffaut, and Resnais. The list of films shown at this little cinema through those years belies the notion that Dublin was a place culturally censored and repressed by the forces loyal to the Catholic archbishop. Although there were a few celebrated cases of direct interference in the theatre, and censorship of films did exist and cuts were made, there was an extraordinary wealth of visual imagery for McGahern to absorb, and so in the years before television or later technologies his eye for visual imagery, for the play of light and shade in the intense space of the cinema, may have left its mark. 'My imagination is primarily visual', he explained in saying that he works with 'a scene in your mind'. 'I see scenes and people in my head all the time, and they move and come to life in words, as do the places in which they live.'[15] Even more pointedly, he referred to 'a cinema that's inside your head that you write out of' and referred to the inner monologue of Elizabeth Reegan in *The Barracks* as a film in slow motion.[16]

'In the summer of 1954 my father remarried. When St. Patrick's closed for the summer, I took the boat for England to look for work on the buildings.'[17] The brevity of these statements masks disillusionments and ambitions that must have crystallized at the end of this first year of creating an adult life for himself. The eldest child's deliberate refusal to attend his father's wedding and his departure from Ireland without communicating with him marked an uncompromising social rejection. In fact, this public humiliation of the father reflects a remarkable strength of character, an assertion of a power and freedom designed to signal that from now on he must no longer be taken for granted in the role of son, that he is set on an independent course according to his own lights. Letters from the father to Rosaleen in London eventually re-establish an indirect line of communication, but this is clearly on the son's terms. The stand-off suggested in these few lines in *Memoir* has depths of anger and aggression, the son countering and neutralizing the father at the end of years of adolescent suffering, and these abrasive actions in the summer of 1954 are certainly coloured by that experience.

The Dark and the unpublished novel 'The End or the Beginning of Love', completed in the late 1950s, depict something of the nature of that suffering in the father's house, but the portrayal of the estranged son, Luke, in *Amongst Women*, surely recaptures some of the bitter feelings of that summer. All through this novel of family intimacy, from the early question 'Where's Luke then?', the uncompromising separation of Luke is reflected on by the other family members: 'it cast a deep shadow when they tried to imagine what kind of space enclosed Luke in England... but they weren't able to imagine it. It was too much like facing darkness.'[18] Over the years depicted in the novel, the absence of Luke remains enigmatic to the family: 'They felt that Luke's whole behaviour was unnatural and hard and unforgiving.'[19] Luke's life in London is not explored in the novel—although McGahern did mention that an extended treatment of it was actually written and edited out—but the absolute silence he establishes between himself and 'Daddy' reflects something of McGahern's struggle with his own vulnerability and violence. *Memoir* documents how he learned to wield a kind of self-protective power to counter the authority of the father, and the departure to London is a centrally symbolic moment in the young man's alienation.

It may be that McGahern also wanted to be free of the ethos of the country. 'The huge waves of organized devotion that marked the Marian Year of 1954 were thought a greater triumph of Irish Catholic and national solidarity than the Eucharistic Congress of

1932.'[20] He was nineteen, and while the tone of this passage suggests that he wanted to escape from the devotional claustrophobia, in these same pages he discusses the steady flow of emigrants to England which had begun to seem normal. The triumphant Irish Catholic nation had abandoned and was being abandoned by a substantial part of its population. Sizeable immigrant communities were growing in many English cities, and in linking up with his sister Rosaleen in London he experienced such a community at first hand. McGahern stayed in St Ann's, a Catholic hostel near Brick Lane in the East End, and worked with a team of Irish labourers on a building site near Aldgate. This was a significant moment when brother and sister met, for it initiated a recreation of the family without the father. At this time, his twin sisters, Rosaleen and Breedge, were in the early stages of their training as nurses and of their settling in Leytonstone in north-east London, where they will marry and raise families.

This summer also introduced McGahern to the experience of exile. He will later show deep sympathy for people uprooted against their will, and the effort to accomplish a reorientation in estrangement will engage him deeply in his fiction. One of his first unpublished fictions is an extended effort to capture that emigrant experience in London. The city came to represent in McGahern's fiction the other place, the place of uncertainty, where so many emigrants had to invent a new life, although still deeply attached to the original home in various parts of rural Ireland. For some, there were lifelines—the provincial newspapers, the regular journeys home, the banding together in Irish groups in pubs and clubs—and these amounted to a surrogate life. He recalled more than once the bitterness he felt in this Irish community. A young Clareman, hearing of the extremely rainy summer in Ireland, remarked, 'May they all have to climb trees. May it rise higher than it did for fukken Noah.' His own anger at the political and economic system that failed to provide for them, that, in fact, excluded them and condescended to them, is palpable and is another key element in his criticism of the bourgeois establishment in Ireland which entered into easy cooperation with a zealous Catholic Church. But it is also evident that London represented a freedom from repression and poverty which many appreciated, among them McGahern and his twin sisters, and, later, his young brother, Frank, and even later, Dympna. All these siblings settled in London, and in later years, McGahern maintained close contact with this extended English-Irish family. He had a striking sensitivity to the complex and often unarticulated emotions of this emigrant community, and after almost fifty years he finally captured this experience in the character of Johnny in *That They May Face the Rising Sun*.

One emigrant he met in the hostel was Tony Whelan. Seven years older than McGahern, he worked in a bookshop, informed himself from weekly reviews of new books and current literary taste and, as he recalled, 'had a more lofty ambition that I had cherished from my schooldays: to become a writer, possibly a great writer'.[21] Soon after they met, Whelan moved to work in a Dublin bookshop, where he remained for three years, during which time he and McGahern met frequently, discussed books—initially the younger man deferring to Whelan's wide experience of literature—and, after Whelan moved back to London, stayed in contact for most of a decade.

While the experience of that first summer in London was undoubtedly difficult—as the draft novel based on those experiences makes clear—*Memoir* suggests that he arrived in a state of high romance. 'Religious feeling does not die easily. When I walked off the boat at Holyhead to the waiting London train—and thought of Shakespeare, Milton, Dickens, all the great English writers I had read and studied—I felt awe, as if I was stepping on to sacred ground.'[22] The import of the opening sentence is unclear; undoubtedly, he is suggesting that his feeling for literature had become a 'religious feeling', transferred from his religious faith, now waning, and that in one form or another 'religious feeling' remains—'does not die'. What is not so clear is if he is critical of that 'awe' he felt, of the canonical power these English writers had, an authority similar to that of the Church, or if, indeed, he is suggesting that the sense of literary England as a 'sacred ground' remained with him long afterwards. It seems to say that, at this time, Literature—where he now anchored his sense of his later identity—was 'the great English writers'. He appears to have felt that he was coming to his true poetic home; to a degree this romantic predisposition appears to have survived even the uncivilized lives to which he was exposed on the building site, a reality he captured later in the story 'Hearts of Oak, Bellies of Brass'.

In *The Barracks*, Elizabeth's awakening through her relationship with Halliday is set in this precise part of the East End of London. It was a literary relationship, as well as a sexual one, for through him she discovers the spiritual liberation of reading. 'She had loved Halliday and had counted no cost. She could feel again her excitement bringing him back the first real books she'd been ever given and crying, "But they're real! They're not stories even. They're about my life"...He had changed her whole life, it was as if he'd put windows there, so that she could see out on her own world.'[23] Indeed, apart from *The Dark*, every novel includes key episodes of major thematic importance set in London. McGahern's affectionate feelings for the city are, perhaps, best captured in Part II of *The Leavetaking*. Patrick Moran experiences a personal liberation when he meets an American girl in the city, falls in love, and when he is fired from his job as a teacher in Dublin, they return to England together.

At the end of his second year at St Pat's, and graduation, McGahern did not take off for London, as he had done the previous summer; neither did he seek out the Bat's services as an unofficial placement officer. Many jobs for the graduating teachers were in his hands to grant to boys who ingratiated themselves in appropriate ways, but McGahern recounts that he was too proud to be under such an obligation. In fact, he seems to have felt considerable ambivalence about becoming a teacher, as the story of a recently graduated young teacher, 'High Ground', suggests, and in a draft of another story he refers to 'some unreadiness or fear or vanity to be named in a way of life'.[24] He hesitated to fall into the sharply defined role he could by now see clearly, with responsibilities he must have known he could not carry out wholeheartedly. 'The life of a teacher was permanently on view in the small parishes, and only in Dublin could I disappear into my own and my secret life without being noticed, but a great number of the other students, for different reasons, also wanted schools in the university towns and cities. I was even thinking of returning to England.'[25] He delayed his decision until the end of the summer and passed the time reroofing his father's newly purchased house at Grevisk, which will be his residence in retirement.

The ambience of this old stone house, formerly a gardener's residence on the Rockingham estate, and close to the Moroneys' house, assumed a symbolic importance for McGahern:

> The land had been the nursery gardens for the Nash house above Lough Key. In its heyday fourteen gardeners worked the fields, and the head gardener lived in the house. There were great trees on the land, exotic plants and flowers brought back from India and China, grass-grown walks. The soil was rich…There was a gate in the high Rockingham wall across the road from the house to a bridle path that led through the woods and pastures all the way to Rockingham House.[26]

This is a nineteenth-century world, a kind of dream landscape that seems connected not to the historical realities of Anglo-Irish landlordism but to Russian fiction, to the world of Turgenev and Tolstoy, and, of course, unmistakably, to the poetry of Yeats. There was a late Georgian grandeur about Rockingham House and the estate that had captivated him when he had visited it years earlier with his father. In 1962, for instance, writing to his editor at the *New Yorker*, he explained some references in the story 'Strandhill, the Sea' by referring to Yeats's *Autobiographies*, and in the case of the Bishop Hudson School he commented: 'It would be a pity to leave out the name, because few such schools remain, leftovers from the Protestant Ascendancy, and they would have the romantic pull of grace and luxury for the boy, and they are also mixed schools, rare in Ireland.'[27]

But if the big house and its 'romantic pull' continued to enchant him through his youth and later, a year after this first visit to Grevisk, the mansion was destroyed by fire, and soon after the estate was divided by the Land Commission into parcels of land for many local farmers. McGahern mentioned the burning many times in future decades, beginning, anachronistically, in *The Barracks*, the actions of which appear to take place about five years earlier. The fire marked the end of an era for him, noted with some nostalgia, it may be, and thirty years later he would return in imagination to this era, in some of the stories of *High Ground* and in *The Rockingham Shoot*. In *Amongst Women*, 'Great Meadow', the house of the 'aristocratic Morans', will retain some of this ambience of the 'old stone house' at Grevisk.

Eventually, McGahern found a teaching position in Athboy, County Meath, and the stories 'Crossing the Line' and 'A Ballad', also written in the early 1980s and included in *High Ground*, are set very precisely in this town.[28] Both of these stories and 'High Ground' reveal considerable ambivalence about entering the profession of teacher and about living in a small town away from the city. During this first year of his teaching career, he transferred at some point to the Christian Brothers' school in Drogheda, but his real goal was to return to Dublin. The following year he began teaching in Scoil Eoin Baiste (Belgrove School) in Clontarf, an old suburb near the centre of Dublin, where he would remain for eight years. His comments on his experience as a teacher and on the place of education in Irish society in the 1950s range widely, but his harshest comments seem to be rooted in this first year, rather than in the Clontarf years. His initiation into the profession appears to have confirmed much of what he suspected from his training:

> I found that teachers in my generation (but then look at the training colleges) were anti-intellectual and philistine; there was a fear of both literature and refinement; the only safe position was the yahoo's position. The trouble was that the Church was anti-intellectual and the Church employed them. They only wanted them to teach Catechism and I think they wanted them servile.[29]

Although the physical building and location depicted in *The Leavetaking* is recognizably the school in Clontarf, the pedagogical situation in which the disaffected Patrick Moran teaches reflects a more literary image of this systemic servility derived from his experience in Athboy or Drogheda. He contrasted the ethos of the Presentation Brothers in Carrick-on-Shannon, which he found liberal, tolerant, and supportive, with the 'unChristian' Brothers in Drogheda.

If 'the yahoo's position' had governed the culture and official discourse of St Pat's, McGahern's story 'A Ballad' explores this small town world in its sexual aspect. One cannot assume that a story written in the 1980s reflects a reality seen and interpreted in these literary terms by the young McGahern in the 1950s, yet there is material here from the time he lived in digs in Athboy which he brought back to life. Not only is the young teacher an observer of the mores of his fellow-boarders in this instance, but it may be that his later remarks on 'the moral climate in which I grew up' are rooted here:

> The confusion and guilt and plain ignorance that surrounded sex turned men and women into exploiters and adversaries. Amid all this, the sad lusting after respectability, sugar-coated with sanctimoniousness and held together by a thin binding of religious doctrine and ceremony, combined to form a very dark and explosive force that, generally, went inward and hid.[30]

He is writing in 1991 with specific reference to his play *The Power of Darkness*, although it may be that the 'dark and explosive force' was in his mind earlier when he wrote *The Dark* in 1963–4, or earlier still; his comments appear to be as apt in describing 'A Ballad' as the play, and the field work on which that story is based goes back to this year, its caustic satire very precisely honed.

In September 1956, McGahern began teaching in Belgrove School. Situated on Seafield Road West, the school is just up from the sea-front park that soon becomes Dollymount as the northern shore of Dublin Bay curves around towards Sutton and Howth. Clontarf is a middle-class suburb, largely consisting of nineteenth-century redbrick homes, and for all his time there McGahern lived in one of these redbrick houses, at 57 Howth Road. His bed-sitting-room became his home in the city, and the many stories and novels that reflect his years in Dublin are as precisely situated in this neigh-bourhood as the fiction set in Cootehall and environs. The time—late 1950s and early 1960s—and the place are scrupulously preserved, in 'My Love, My Umbrella', 'Sierra Leone', *The Pornographer*, and *The Leavetaking*. The school, the pubs around Fairview Park, the walk and the bus route into the centre of the city, the sea, are all evoked as a familiar environment in which a young man's sentimental edu-cation is traced, explorations in sex and love take place, a sensibility is defined.

McGahern wrote that 'the years that followed were slow and full and sometimes difficult', but in the memoir they are sketched in a few scattered paragraphs, about five pages of the fifty devoted to the family narrative of the late 1950s. It appears that his teaching and the organization of his time were actually close to what he had envisaged. In some ways, his experience in Belgrove School was the opposite of what he had known in the Christian Brothers in Drogheda. The ambience in the school appears to have been reasonably congenial, although he found the teaching onerous—'if you do anything well, or you try to do anything well, it's hard work and it's painful'. In *Memoir* he identified what is hard about teaching: 'to bend young minds from their animal instincts and interest them in combinations of words and numbers and histories'.[31] He seems to accept that a conflict of wills is involved, and the firm imposition of discipline necessary, but in this aspect of the task, it appears that for the most part, he had the clear authority of parents supporting him. Some of his former pupils have recorded impressions of him as a teacher; some found his discipline harsh and his presence intimidating, while others recalled that he communicated a passion for storytelling and literature. *Memoir* also conveys a sense of the satisfaction of the job: 'seeing the work take root and grow, encouraging the weaker children so that they grow in trust and confidence, seeing them all emerge as individuals'. It is a textbook statement of pedagogical goals, but, in fact, his own evolution can be sensed in these words, for at this stage nothing was as important for himself as the attainment of his own confident individuality. In this school, he seems to have settled into a career that was close to what he needed for that other work: 'Once the children ran free from the school at two fifteen in the afternoon, the rest of the day was my own.' It was what he had recognized as the condition that would enable him as a teacher to pursue his 'secret vocation'.

In spite of his growing sense of how that individuality may be founded in dissent and opposition, McGahern appears to have negotiated the obligations to teach Irish and religion without great difficulty. 'In school I taught the catechism and led the children in the obligatory prayers with the same ease as when I believed.'[32] Over and above the private matter of conscience, he dissented from the extent to which these subjects were the core of the education the children received. Whatever the actual distribution of time in the teacher's day—he reports variously that more than 50 per cent had to be devoted to Irish and religion—the overwhelming emphasis is what he resented. The educational system reflected the biases of the

official cultural ethos and neglected the kind of individual empowerment for their future lives that pupils should gain from education.

How soon he came to articulate the grounds of his dissent and the
severe judgement he would later pass on the post-revolutionary
society and cultural ethos is uncertain, but there is little doubt that
it formed through these years and was clear by the time he came to
write *The Barracks* and *The Dark*. It will inform much of his fiction—
The Leavetaking, most notably, and later *Amongst Women*—but, starting
in the 1980s, he began to spell out his dissent in non-fictional declarations. 'A nation or society which does not place education at the
very forefront of its values will soon have no sense of itself apart
from what Freud calls "narcissistic illusion". Without knowledge we
can have no sense of tradition which must be continually renewed,
and tradition is civilization.'[33] It is evident that his experience as a
teacher contributed to this belief that the institutionalized 'tradition'
was not a real 'civilization'; rather, it was a 'narcissistic illusion' of
nationhood. The severity of such judgements emerged much later,
when terms like 'manners' and 'civilization' became common, but
the reading of Freud's *The Future of an Illusion* may have coloured his
thinking as early as the late 1950s. In fact, it may be difficult to
separate McGahern's thinking about authoritarian mentalities and
narcissism in the culture as a whole from his efforts to come to terms
with his own father's abusive character. This association of narcissism and revolt is a central strand of the narrative told in *Memoir*; as
far as education and the development of a confident sense of self is
concerned, however, he seems to make a crucial distinction: 'People,
especially young people, will find ways around a foolish system, and
difficulty can often serve to sharpen desire, but many who could not
were damaged or were driven into damaged lives.'[34] He was obviously a survivor of a 'foolish system', one whose education was not
an obstacle in his fulfilment of desire, yet his fiction is deeply rooted
in a keen sense of what 'damaged lives' feel like, and how the
Ireland of the time bred deep bitterness and frustration in the lives
of many.

His ease at the school in Clontarf may be partly attributable to the
presence of two older colleagues who became friends. Both these men
had mature interests in literature, were keen readers, and one of them
was an established writer in the Irish language. Tom Jordan had been

a Christian Brother who had left the order, although not the Church; he became a close and lifelong friend of McGahern. Another colleague, Donncha Ó Céileachair, a prolific and highly regarded writer of short stories and non-fiction in Irish, also became a friend. Ó Céileachair was more than a decade older than McGahern, and a fervent Catholic. In the year before McGahern arrived in the school, Ó Céileachair had published *Bullaí Mhártain*, a celebrated collection of stories written with his sister. Both of them had met Daniel Corkery, the most prominent literary figure then in the city of Cork, and were inspired by him. Although the friendship with Ó Céileachair developed in the school environment—where it seems literary conversations took place in the playground while supervising the boys—it may be surmised that a classic in Irish such as Tomás Ó Criomhthain's *An tOileánach/ The Islandman*, already known to McGahern as a required school text, might have taken on a real literary significance through this friendship. Perhaps more than anything else, Ó Céileachair was the model of what McGahern wished to become, a teacher who was also a disciplined and productive writer. Here was 'the dream' in action.

'My life in the Dublin of the time would not have been much different to the lives of many young men', McGahern wrote in a passage designed to make his distinctive life almost invisible:

> We worked. We went to dancehalls and cinemas and theatres; the big hurling and football matches in Croke Park, race meetings in the Phoenix Park or Baldoyle or Leopardstown; we met and talked and drank and argued in bars. In hot summers we swam in the seas around Dublin or went on excursions into the Dublin mountains. The girls we picked up in dancehalls we courted in doorways and back alleys, and on dates took them to cinemas or out to places like Howth by the sea.[35]

While all this is undoubtedly true, as far as it goes, it seems to stand for the many years when he led a 'normal' life, that is before he became a writer, even though that is what he wanted to be. Yet the kind of writer he became is also marked by an effort to preserve the centrality of 'normal' experience, in the face of what was clearly the extraordinary experience that made him need to be a writer, as well as the outstanding talent as a reader which enriched his imagination and enabled him to begin writing and to find a style.

His general statements in the following paragraph about the Ireland of the time—'an Irish society that was childish, repressive and sectarian'—suggest that what he wanted to value as 'normal' was also marked by severely dislocating ideologies and beliefs. There is an important tension here between what is said to be abnormal as part of a historical analysis and the common behaviour of the 'young men' of the culture in which McGahern felt comfortably integrated. Already, in the glimpse of boarding-house life in Athboy, there is a suggestion that the young man in the room overhead set himself apart from the 'yahoos' downstairs; yet to alienate oneself from the common experience, to distance oneself too far from the 'normal', may be to risk a loss of moral stability. This would be a central theme of *The Pornographer*, but *Memoir* insists that in these years he was almost indistinguishable from other young men.

Stories and novels set in Dublin provide rich evidence of how McGahern immersed himself in the sights and sounds, the sensual and spiritual possibilities of the city from the beginning. In all those different ways, he was exploring:

> The distractions of the city quickened forgetting, the excitement of books for the first time, no longer the dull slog for exams but ways of seeing, one's own world for the first time. The laughter and argument of pubs, and late at night the dances, girls from the dances, and fumbled sex in the back seats of cars or on bed-sitting room sofas or against alley walls, wet trouser legs and the stiff grey stain that had to be sent to the cleaners'.[36]

This passage of summary comes from *The Leavetaking*, but there are many scattered details in stories and elsewhere which confirm that fiction and recollection are closely allied. Speaking of his first love, the virginal girl from County Leitrim who reminded him of his mother, and the end of that relationship, he writes, 'I ran from the shadow and the country dream it withered, by way of small town schools, each move bringing me closer to the city.' And in the city there will be sex and love affairs which will not always be inhibited by Catholic puritanism. The girls, the bars, the street life all became as real to his imagination as the life of Cootehall or Carrick-on-Shannon.

If original dreams and memories were associated with country places, the reality of the city and its possibilities became the place in which he would forge a new identity. In his references to this time, one detail stands out as emblematic: the second-hand book-barrow on Henry Street:

> Most of the books the barrow carried would now be described as modern classics...Books were discussed and argued about around the barrow; intellectual women could be met there, and there was no man more alert to the sexual possibilities of these encounters than Mr. Kelly. Though he had a wife and a large family in the suburbs, was a devout Catholic, a Republican and a racist, he observed no contradiction once his self-interest or pleasure came into play.[37]

The details provide a vivid glimpse not only of Mr Kelly but of his observer, for this mingling of books, sex, and talk in a haphazard urban setting provided an exciting sense of possibility and adventure. The profile of Mr Kelly, revealed to be an IRA activist, situates this larger-than-life character and his ambience in an episode out of Dickens. In fact, Dublin and London, McGahern's first cities, would be joined by Paris and Barcelona as other favourite cities later in the decade, and in time there would be others, as he became a keen traveller. From this time and for perhaps twenty years, his life would be anchored in the pleasures and possibilities of city life. He had to make a willed effort to turn away from his past life as a child, to gain imaginative and emotional distance from it, and to gain an adult urban experience, before he could, as he will, return to the country in the 1970s on his own terms.

What McGahern was discovering, then, through his own explorations, was that the real life of the city opened to reveal a very different world from the one he had known and had been led to imagine through the official pronouncements of Church and State. The official cultural images of Ireland and Irishness, the careful controlling of debate and discussion, the censorship of ideas, the interpretations of Ireland's history presented in schools, all came to seem like a fantasy. His writing began and was rooted in an acknowledgement of the truth of experience: 'Everything begins in experience, how could one know anything unless one had experience? I think of writing as drawing or painting, so I keep close to the way things actually happened.'[38] And so this acute observer and recorder of his own intimate experience growing up became an equally acute observer of the reality in which he found himself.

McGahern's fictional Dublin has an authenticity of detail that rivals Joyce's and is clear evidence of how he welcomed the opportunities for immersion in city life—in fact, how he came to love the city. One of those who became a close friend in the next decade was the Dubliner Kevin Lehane, author of a series of vivid articles in the *Irish Times* on traditional Dublin life and speech that gave McGahern 'much pleasure'. These articles were written under the pseudonym Tom Corkery and were published as a book in 1980. McGahern reviewed *Tom Corkery's Dublin*, and his lovingly chosen excerpts of pub conversation indicate how Lehane must have been the perfect guide to his city. 'They stand both the test of collection and time with remarkable freshness. They are quiet, shrewd, sly, affectionate, traditional, unobtrusively skilful and, above all, humorous. They celebrate place and character and custom, are as thronged and full of good things as their beloved Moore and Henry Streets on a busy Saturday.'[39] In his professional life, Lehane was manager of a large cinema on O'Connell Street where McGahern was frequently his guest in the dining room, but Lehane's valued companionship was the result not only of his easy immersion in the textures of the daily life of the city but in his artistic ability to capture those textures. The terms of McGahern's appreciation of Lehane's writing sound very close to a shorthand for the qualities he would aim for in his own work.

It would be an artificial formula to suggest that, in coming to love the city, he separated himself entirely from his original rural culture: far from it. Again, the stories of his return home to his father's house and the blending of home and city in such stories as 'Wheels', 'Sierra Leone', and 'Goldwatch' reveal the acute tension he experienced and was capable of dramatizing. *Memoir* provides ample evidence of the close and fraught relationship with his father during this decade. What it does not reveal is how he was interpreting his urban experience, how he was situating himself in this cultural milieu, and how it was contributing to the sensibility that will later be made concrete in words.

3

'The years of training in the secret Dublin years'

The literary milieu in which McGahern found himself in Dublin was one in which literature really mattered, not only to its practitioners and their readers but also in the general cultural discourse of national self-consciousness. The Irish Literary Revival of two generations before had been identified largely with W. B. Yeats and his associates, in founding the Abbey Theatre, for instance, and with the kind of enabling rediscovery for poetry and drama of the ancient and indigenous Celtic myths. The legends and folklore of country people, especially in the West of Ireland, and the notion of an uncorrupted peasantry, had inspired Yeats, his followers, and political activists who saw cultural revival as part of a wider movement for decolonization. But from the beginning in the 1890s and up to the 1950s, there were promoters of a more Gaelic and Catholic Ireland who saw Yeats as an inauthentic Irishman of Anglo-Irish and Protestant background who was, consciously or unconsciously, too sympathetic to British imperial attitudes. A prominent nationalist ideologue like Daniel Corkery argued the case for inauthenticity, although Seán O'Faolain and Frank O'Connor, Corkery's former friends, and guerrilla fighters in the war of independence and the civil war, were admirers of Yeats in the 1930s and, to a degree, received his blessing as the definitive writers of post-Independence Ireland. In spite of controversy—and Yeats welcomed it in his role as Senator when he spoke out against censorship and against Catholic-inspired social legislation, such as the prohibition of divorce— he presided over Irish writing as an elder statesman and quotable lyric poet. In the decades after his death, Yeats continued to be a vital literary presence.

In contrast, in the early 1950s, the work of Joyce was unknown to the general public, and, for instance, was not on school curricula in Ireland, even at third level. *Ulysses* was available only under the counter and, in general in literary circles, Joyce's work was not considered celebratory of, or sympathetic to, the national spirit. The same might be said of other writers, such as Wilde, Shaw, and O'Casey. Some of the early plays of O'Casey—*The Shadow of a Gunman*, *Juno and the Paycock*, and *The Plough and the Stars*—were often produced in Dublin theatres, but his communist sympathies and his anti-Catholic sentiments ensured that he was an alienated figure. The verbal and imaginative exuberance of Joyce and O'Casey were admired by a core audience, but the Catholic establishment marked them out more generally as enemies of the Church and the nation. The protection of an image of the uncorrupted and incorruptible 'Catholic people' had been a recurring feature of national discourse from the riots over *The Playboy of the Western World* in 1907 right up to the 1950s. Two highly publicized controversies blew up in that decade when John Charles McQuaid, the Archbishop of Dublin, tried to have new plays banned. O'Faolain and O'Connor were known as realists and both spoke out strongly against censorship—many of their own books had been banned in the 1930s and 1940s—but they remained cultural nationalists, engaged in criticizing along liberal republican lines a conservative and repressive state.

Figures like Patrick Kavanagh and Flann O'Brien had introduced very different dimensions to considerations of the artistic life by aligning themselves in ways that were outside the literary/political discourse. Even though Kavanagh was a poet of the country in his work of the 1930s and 1940s—*Ploughman and Other Poems*, his memoir *The Green Fool*, and the novel *Tarry Flynn*—he was by no means a follower of the Literary Revival, nor did he present a pious view of the Irish peasantry. His long poem *The Great Hunger* provided the most naked view of Irish rural frustration and repression ever written, and it was instantly suppressed. Kavanagh rejected Irishness as a literary critical concept in favour of an idea of the poet as seer and prophet, working in a more timeless and stateless zone. Flann O'Brien/Myles na Gopaleen wrote in postmodern and satirical styles—even in Irish—which embodied an anarchistic and angry individualism. These writers and their supporters in Ireland were decidedly at odds with the romanticized image of peasant life as an artistic and moral norm; they were urban, modern, eclectic, and not followers of any established political or religious agenda.

McGahern appears to have quickly found his bearings in this literary-critical discourse. Through his friendship with Éanna Ó hEither, his attendance at the Gate Theatre and art cinemas, and his sceptical dissent from the Gaelic and Catholic ambience of St Pat's, he was already set on a cultural path away from the mainstream. His eclectic reading was markedly European in its emphasis throughout the 1950s: Dostoevsky, Thomas Mann, Proust, Chekhov, and other classic writers will be common reference points by the end of the decade. Although he did not know Joyce's name when he arrived in Dublin in 1953, he would soon move in a milieu in which Joyce's work was revered. As he said later, he himself was inevitably Irish and could not be anything else, but to belabour the point or to adopt a self-conscious agenda of furthering some nationalist political or cultural agenda was anathema to him from the beginning. And he will find his own way of reading Yeats and of becoming a writer of the country. Good writing, clear thinking, deep feeling were his critical categories, and wherever he found such writing in the broader field of European literature, he began to feel his way towards his own sense of tradition. As he remarked much later, 'I became a writer by accident, and I didn't grow up in any tradition. In fact, it's a question of whether there is a literary tradition in Ireland, no matter what is made out of it, because I think that tradition is individualistic rather than *a* tradition.'[1]

Towards the end of 1955, a chance meeting with Tony Swift, a young painter, set McGahern's life along an entirely new track. *Memoir* relates that the meeting happened in the bar of a dancehall, and that it led to his introduction into the Swift family and their home on Carrick Terrace, off Dublin's South Circular Road. Five brothers ran a display advertising business, with a factory near Amiens Street railway station, and in time, when he moved back to Dublin, he would become part of this large, closely knit family. He referred affectionately to both the parents. Two of the brothers were of especial interest to him, and in different ways they played significant roles in his early development.[2]

James was the eldest, ten years older than McGahern. 'When I went to Dublin', McGahern told an interviewer, 'I met a person who had a deep, passionate sense of literature, who put many true books in my way, but he was far too intelligent to encourage anyone to write.'[3] He is undoubtedly referring to Jimmy Swift. Jimmy had been in the Irish army before setting up the business with his brothers, and in addition to his great passion for literature and his promotion of 'true books'—to his brothers as much as to McGahern—his character and temperament are also significant. His younger brother provided a sketch to illustrate the 'extraordinary evenness of his behaviour at all times':

> I was always getting into some stupid row or other in the house, attacking someone, shouting, just being a terrible nuisance, until Jimmy would have to take charge and physically throw me out into the street. An hour or so later I'd feel miserable, ashamed of my life to meet Jimmy, feeling horrible. He'd just smile as if nothing at all had taken place and ask if I'd be interested in wandering down to McCauley's for a drink.[4]

While this sketch introduces the volatile brother, Patrick, as one who liked argument, debate, conflict of ideas, it introduces James as a benign and constant father-surrogate. McGahern entered into a lifelong friendship with James, 'quietly brilliant and deeply read', and the significance of this early friendship is marked by the dedication of *The Barracks* to him.

Like his brother, Jimmy Swift was a fluent talker about literary and artistic ideas. For many years, he and McGahern met at the Stag's Head pub to discuss books—McGahern, as if obliquely recalling his meeting with the Swifts, commented that 'these were times when books were discussed in dancehalls as well as in bars'. When McGahern wrote in *Memoir* that his friend was 'quietly brilliant', he may have meant that, unlike his brother Patrick, Jimmy never wrote or published anything, but he was someone whose belief in literature made a forceful impact. It was he who introduced McGahern to the work of Proust, for instance, and, as if in thanks, the novelist includes in 'Wheels' and *The Leavetaking* a character, Lightfoot, who meets the protagonist in the Stag's Head and is a Proustian. One must assume that his introduction was a forceful and enthusiastic one, for Proust would become a touchstone for much in McGahern's writing and his thinking about writing, and this remained true from the 1950s until the end of his life.

Patrick was a painter, seven years older than McGahern, and had lived in London much of the time since 1952, but his early interests and contacts in Dublin led, through James, to McGahern's familiarity with a literary circle that would overlap other literary circles in Dublin and London over the next decade. Patrick Swift had graduated from the National College of Art and immediately established himself as a significant painter, with work shown at the Irish Exhibition of Living Art in 1950. In addition to painting, he had wide intellectual and literary interests, which he shared in a highly articulate manner in pubs and in print. The origin of his passion for literature lay in Synge Street school, where he and his close friend John Jordan discovered *Ulysses* at the age of sixteen.[5] 'If you look at Joyce's career', McGahern said in the 1980s, 'it shows a real difference between the city and the country. He was reading Henry James and people like that when he was fifteen or sixteen. There was no chance, if he was living in the country, that he would have been doing that.'[6] McGahern is probably misremembering Joyce's celebrated discovery of Ibsen at a young age, but it is also likely that he is recalling the precociousness of Swift and Jordan. In any case, it seems that he felt at a disadvantage vis-à-vis city youths and that he appreciated this opportunity to catch up. In their youth, Swift and Jordan devoted themselves to Joyce's work for some time, both attached to the novelist of Dublin whose work seemed to bring their home place to surreal life. Swift memorized passages of *Finnegans Wake* and *Ulysses*, and at an early age he became a well-known personality in literary pubs, with a prodigious memory for quotation from many literary classics. In art college, he had befriended John Ryan, who became the editor/publisher of *Envoy*, a short-lived but very significant literary review in 1949–51, where Swift's first essays on art were published.

It was in this context of *Envoy* that Swift met Patrick Kavanagh (for the promotion of whose work, it might be said, John Ryan had established *Envoy*) and other young writers who were devotees of Kavanagh, such as Anthony Cronin. Cronin was an assistant editor of *The Bell* and would later, throughout the 1950s and 1960s, work in London publishing circles where he befriended many poets, critics, and painters, a circle that included Patrick Swift for about a decade, Francis Bacon, Lucian Freud, and the South African poet David Wright. Little magazines flourished in these years, in Dublin and in London, and McGahern quickly realized that they were a key part of establishing a literary presence.

In time, McGahern would meet, and linger with, many of these figures, and think carefully about their work, and consider too the real value of literary coteries for his life's work, but at this point, in 1956, the young teacher was extraordinarily lucky to find a door opening into this circle. He referred to the 'living, exciting presences in the city' of Beckett and Kavanagh because of the new work which appeared in the magazines: 'I wish I could open a magazine now with the same excitement.'[7] In particular, he was thinking of *Nimbus*, edited by Wright for a few years in the mid-1950s; his awareness of it was focused in an exciting way in the early months of 1956 because a supplement on Kavanagh's work was being planned, and the Swift brothers had a special role in this.[8]

While Kavanagh was a prominent presence in literary pubs around Baggot Street and Grafton Street, often an aggressive and abrasive bohemian, he was also seen as the uncompromising figure of the ideal poet. On a visit from London in January 1956, Patrick Swift discovered that Kavanagh had an embryonic collection in a grubby typescript—many poems from *Envoy* and some later poems. He persuaded the poet to part with it and, on his departure, left his brother Jimmy with the responsibility of having clean copies typed, one to be forwarded to David Wright, editor of *Nimbus*. The original typescript was autographed and given to Jimmy Swift, and this is how John McGahern was swept up in the excitement of this revival of Kavanagh's career. At the Swifts' house, he read the poems in manuscript before a sizeable selection appeared in the London quarterly. His impassioned involvement with these poems of Kavanagh was intensified in March 1956 when he attended with Jimmy Swift some of the extramural lectures the poet was giving at University College Dublin. One memorable line he remembered was the analogy of the sonnet as an envelope for love, but it is clear that he was greatly taken by Kavanagh's verbal flair, his 'wild swing', and his powerful conviction of the spiritual significance of poetry. However much time he and his friend Jimmy Swift spent in Kavanagh's difficult company—and McGahern would later write about those difficulties and write of Kavanagh's life and work with sympathetic detachment—it is certain that from the beginning of 1956 and for some time afterwards, the poems, and later *The Great Hunger* and *Tarry Flynn*, greatly excited him and undoubtedly provided him with a sense of the dedicated poet as model.

Over the years, McGahern would consider the character of the poet, and learn something of the literary life from his observations, but it was the voice of Kavanagh in the poems published in *Nimbus* in April 1956 that he remembered and which he responded to deeply. It is easy to see why the poems 'Auditors In', 'Prelude', 'Kerr's Ass', and 'The Hospital' would have had this effect, although there are other significant poems too. Later, in his writing about Kavanagh, he focused on the poems, many of which he would continue to admire all his life, and, separately, on Kavanagh's character as artist and person. His earliest excitement is attributable to the magisterial, if self-deprecating, persona: 'He had an individual vision, a vigorous gift for catching the rhythms of ordinary speech, and he was able to bring the images that move us into the light, without patronage and on an equal footing with any great work.'[9] McGahern might have been summing up his own gifts, for at this stage, in mid-career, these are the attributes he would speak of in revealing his own artistic persona. He is offering his definition of the unique talent and power of a 'great' artist; the extent to which his definition is a retrospective one or was actually formed by his reading of Kavanagh can hardly be decided. At any rate, this formulation suggests what may have absorbed him as he read.

'To bring the images that move us into the light'; it is McGahern's constant motto. There is no doubt that Kavanagh's images drawn from small-farm life in County Monaghan, the countryside of his childhood, moved McGahern. The depiction of country life would always be central to McGahern's work, and he contrasts Kavanagh's search for authentic expression with the 'phoniness of emotion' of other fashionably 'rural' poets, dismissing the poems of Padraic Colum, 'one of the staples of schoolbooks', as 'emotional vacuity'. Such language reveals that McGahern felt that the 'true voice' of

Kavanagh was rooted in a sincere and deep feeling for his own small world. In 'Auditors In', he read:

> Your imagination still enthuses
> Over the dandelions at Willie Hughes's
> And these are equally valid
> For urban epic, peasant ballad.
> Not mere memory but the Real
> Poised in the poet's commonweal.
> And you must take yourself in hand
> And dig and ditch your authentic land.[10]

From *The Barracks* to *That They May Face the Rising Sun*, McGahern's career would 'dig and ditch your authentic land', but in these lines he must have been moved by much else, in particular by the association of memory and 'the Real'. In fact, a later story, 'Parachutes', uses Kavanagh's image of dandelions in a context associated with him, a pub off Grafton Street, and that story is only one work of fiction among others where Kavanagh's presence can be felt; it is a story that investigates the search for 'the Real' and explores this conflation of 'urban epic, peasant ballad' which was central to Kavanagh's poetic identity at this time. The story is unmistakably a late tribute to and criticism of Kavanagh and his milieu.

The images that moved McGahern were vivid evocations of farm life, of the psychological landscape in joy and desolation, of the 'local row' that could be envisioned as Homeric epic, or of the poet's 'going inland' to discover how his urban epic might be written. The autobiographical play in these poems must surely have engaged him for Kavanagh took great risks with baring his own soul. In 'Prelude' McGahern read:

> And you must go inland and be
> Lost in compassion's ecstasy,
> Where suffering soars in summer air—
> The millstone has become a star.[11]

The casual tone, the apparent indifference, the comic spirit that animates the voice in so many of these poems has an undertow of suffering and desolation. McGahern undoubtedly read 'In Memory of My Mother', an early poem of Kavanagh's which echoes in *Memoir*:

> I do not think of you lying in the wet clay
> Of a Monaghan graveyard; I see
> You walking down a lane among the poplars
> On your way to the station, or happily
>
> Going to second Mass on a summer Sunday—
> [...] And you smile up at us—eternally.[12]

He would know from Jimmy Swift that Kavanagh had suffered from lung cancer in 1955, and the poem 'The Hospital' reflects on that experience. It certainly looks forward to *The Barracks* in lines such as these: 'Naming these things is the love-act and its pledge; / For we must record love's mystery without claptrap, / Snatch out of time the passionate transitory.'[13] Such lines are close to the heart of McGahern's vision in his first novel, and it is clear that, as 'a way of seeing', the novel incorporates much of Kavanagh's sense of suffering, time, and mysteries of the spiritual life and eternity. The sense of poetry as a form of prayer and of the god-like imagination transforming the ordinary into the sacred is evident throughout these poems in *Nimbus*, and this is certainly something that McGahern's work will share. He will refer to both *The Barracks* and *The Dark* as religious works.

While McGahern had his own direct response to the poems he read in manuscript at the Swifts' house, when *Nimbus* appeared a few months later, the poems were accompanied by an essay by Anthony Cronin. Cronin's critical acuity had been in evidence since *Envoy*, and he had been associated with Kavanagh from then on, but the breadth of his reading clearly impressed McGahern, for some of the thinking Cronin drew on in his evaluation of Kavanagh would become central parts of McGahern's own critical vocabulary in later years. In particular, Cronin's spirited outlining of Kavanagh's commitment to the 'poetic repose and contemplation which is at the heart of the satire' seems to anticipate later declarations: 'The movement of poetry is from the particular to the universal, from the ordinary to the significant, and in neither case is there a short cut.' Kavanagh's poetry of the country and the city is valued because it has 'the supreme virtues of humility and honesty'.[14] There is much of Baudelaire in the underlying poetic, and McGahern refers more than once to Baudelaire's remark on technique quoted by Cronin: 'He that possesses nothing but technique is but a beast, while the imagination that attempts to dispense with technique is insane.' The young man from the country may have felt awe as well as ambivalence about the learning of others, of those who, like Swift and Cronin, did not hesitate to display their extensive reading in critical formulations. Certainly in later years he would make a virtue of wearing learning lightly in public, he rarely showed off his extensive reading, and incorporated quotations from classical writers as if they were part of a common wisdom, but in his first decade these contacts may have encouraged him to make use of a more rarefied artistic persona. He would encounter Anthony Cronin and John Jordan in Dublin and London over the next years until he left Dublin in 1964, but both appear to be victims of a satirical treatment in 'Parachutes'; these years, until the writing of *The Barracks*, were years of apprenticeship, and his contacts with such writers were part of his education in the literary life.[15]

How often McGahern may have come back to the *Nimbus* poems (later collected in *Come Dance with Kitty Stobling*) and *The Great Hunger* with a critical sense of how his own work might learn from them is unclear, but his awakening to the presence of a powerful poetic talent in Dublin dates from this moment in early 1956. His trust in Kavanagh's poetic voice would later cool, but the reason for the young man's early attraction to the poems is clear. In his single-minded ambition, as he embarked on 'my training in all those secret Dublin years', continued reflection on Patrick Kavanagh's work and person would remain close to the centre of McGahern's self-education.

McGahern recalled in 'The Solitary Reader' in 1991 that Patrick Kavanagh was one of the 'two living writers who meant most' to him and his friends in the 1950s, and he identified the other as Samuel Beckett. What these two very different artists 'meant' to him in these first years of his development and how their significance evolved through these years up to the writing of *The Barracks* is difficult to document, but a decade later he will name them as key representatives of two traditions in Irish writing 'in their continuance'. He included Kavanagh's *Collected Poems* and *Tarry Flynn*, and Beckett's *Murphy* or *Malone Dies* and *All That Fall* on a reading list for students in January 1969, and explained their inclusion in this way.[16] The phrase is surely a clue to his recognition of these writers' lasting importance to his own growing body of work.

It is remarkable that they entered his awareness almost simultaneously, and in rather dramatic fashion, in the first months of 1956: Kavanagh in person, and Beckett, the figure of the exiled and invisible artist, in the form of an enigmatic and highly successful play, *Waiting for Godot*. The success of *En attendant Godot* in Paris in 1953 led immediately to plans for a production in English, but there were delays so that it did not go on in London until mid-1955; its first Dublin production was at the Pike at the end of the year, and after a sell-out run it transferred to the Gate Theatre and then toured the country. As a regular at both the Pike and the Gate, McGahern saw the play soon after it began its run. It was already the talk of the town. Patrick Kavanagh went to see it numerous times in January 1956 and wrote enthusiastically about it in the *Irish Times*. Its producer, Alan Simpson, argued that the play had a special appeal in Ireland because of its mixed genre of tragi-comedy and the absurd, and many turns of phrase struck Irish ears as very local.[17]

To begin with, McGahern's affection for Beckett may be partially due to his ear for Irish speech, and on a number of later occasions he showed an appreciation of Beckett's comic awareness of ironic and grotesque textures in the vernacular, and, indeed, of ways in which speech takes on a comic life of its own in puns and double entendres. He commented on an episode in *Murphy* as being 'very Irish, very Becketty', and mentioned that Beckett is full of 'comic sayings' like those he himself made use of in *The Barracks*; he saw in Beckett someone who had recognized the amount of 'word-play' that is common in Irish speech and made use of it for his own aesthetic purposes.[18] Later in the decade, perhaps after hearing *All That Fall* on radio, in 1957, by which time Beckett's post-war prose had been translated and published in English, McGahern devoted the intense kind of reading to the work which will leave him with a lifelong admiration for Beckett. The impact of that reading will become evident in the writing of *The Barracks*, *The Dark*, and certain stories in *Nightlines*, but at this moment, in early 1956, Beckett may have assumed a certain emblematic presence in McGahern's reading of the Irish and European literary landscape.

Beckett's early fiction of the 1930s and his essay on Proust were known to a very small number of people in Dublin and, even though he had lived outside Ireland for more than twenty years, he maintained some links and had visited the city from time to time up to the death of his mother in 1950. Old friends such as Thomas MacGreevy and Con Leventhal were known to be in touch with the reclusive writer, and so a younger generation, including Patrick Swift, had become interested in him, in part because he had known Joyce well and had lingered in his entourage in the Paris of the late 1920s and 1930s. *Irish Writing*, a post-war review, and *Envoy* both published work by Beckett. Brendan Behan and other visiting Irish writers made efforts to penetrate his world in the *quartier latin*, but while Beckett would meet them for an evening of drinking in his favourite bar, and continued to do so through the 1950s and 1960s, he maintained an austere image as a dedicated artist, entirely apart from all contemporary influences and pressures, and notably disdainful of cultural nationalism and ways of linking art to its social contexts.

After Joyce, Beckett's exacting dedication to finding a style beyond Anglo-Irish history and literary tradition won him recognition internationally. His work was unique, but it came from Paris, and the cultural glamour associated with that location was an element in the success of *Waiting for Godot*. While the city in the 1920s had become home to an international community of painters, musicians, poets, sculptors, film-makers and novelists—and McGahern would later speak of his love of the American writers in that set, Hemingway and Fitzgerald—the post-war years had a distinctively French identity. In particular, Sartre and Camus had attracted widespread attention for their philosophical work, their fiction, and their plays, all of which appeared to exemplify fundamental tenets of existentialism, and so terms like the Absurd, Nothingness, and Existence became commonplace as the diction of a post-war zeitgeist. Beckett did not set out to expound any philosophical orientation, and certainly not the ideas of Sartre or Camus, but together with Ionescu and others he was situated for a time in this Parisian ambience and in this philosophical vocabulary. Unlike *Nausea* or *The Outsider*, *Waiting for Godot* has no clear dialogue with philosophical ideas or traditions; in fact, it might be said that it subverts all ideas and philosophical systems and returns to remarkably pristine images and a poetic diction that communicate independently of ideas. But it may have been the freedom exemplified by Beckett to become an artist in his own way that struck McGahern, exile in Paris being an enabling foundation, as it had been for many artists and philosophers.

Peter Lennon, a friend of McGahern from Dublin, settled in Paris in the mid-1950s and became an interpreter of French culture and politics throughout the 1960s for *The Guardian*. Lennon was rigorously left-wing in his critical reporting of French politics, as he was in exposing the Irish state's subservience to the Church. He eventually wrote a memoir of these years, during which McGahern visited him on many occasions.[19] Lennon came to be a drinking pal of Beckett; a staunch supporter of McGahern's *The Dark* in 1965–6, it was Lennon who had Beckett read it with a view to endorsing a protest. McGahern did not wish Beckett to do so, but Lennon included references to the McGahern case in his celebrated documentary *The Rocky Road to Dublin*. While McGahern probably did not go far in subscribing to Lennon's political convictions, the world in which Lennon moved was a liberating one imaginatively and intellectually; most of all, it reflected a free cultural space in which a writer like Beckett could work in peace and privacy. His image was that of a secular and disenchanted saint with profound yearnings for meaning and spiritual enlightenment but with a nihilistic and sceptical temperament. His isolation in Paris was a symptom and a source of his art; his struggles with language and expression, teasing poetic nuance out of the plainest vocabulary, seemed to represent a cleansing of literary diction and a return to the most primal aspects of utterance.

To what extent Lennon may have guided McGahern's reading is unclear, but McGahern's early interest in French films is an indication that he was already becoming a Francophile and very likely an explorer of French literature in translation. Apart from the established classic writers, Proust and Flaubert, Baudelaire and Chateaubriand, there are references later to a wide and eclectic range of writing: for instance, Céline's *A Journey to the End of the Night*—one of 'the greatest works of our century'—and Montherlant's *Chaos and Night*. Notable in his absence is François Mauriac, prominent apologist for a Catholic and conservative France at this time, but the lack of reference to him is not clear evidence that McGahern did not read any of his novels; on the contrary, it is more than likely that he did. In fact, a curious comparison of Kavanagh and Céline recalls this time when the young McGahern was exploring in many philosophical and imaginative directions and may indeed have found it possible to embrace many different orientations at once. Writing on the effect of censorship in Ireland, he noted, 'We could appreciate Kavanagh's "Posterity has no use / For anything but the soul, / The lines that speak the passionate heart, / The spirit that lives alone" all the more because we knew Céline's powerful and equally true refutation: "Invoking Posterity is like making speeches to worms".'[20] In insisting that he and his friends were not imaginatively inhibited or restricted by censorship, he sets up a contrast between the 'provincial' religious poet and the nihilistic French memoirist, and there is surely a clue here that his imaginative sympathies reached from the closed worlds of Leitrim and Roscommon to the liberated ambience of post-war Paris.

The Barracks certainly explores philosophical ideas in the meditations of Elizabeth Reegan and explores also certain ways of thinking and believing, and indeed, as in Beckett and others, the operations of mind and consciousness. McGahern's imagination was drawn towards ideas, many of them current in this Parisian context, but he was determined not to subscribe to any system or to appear to endorse a particular intellectual position. While he certainly read Camus and admired *The Outsider* and the essays on the Mediterranean coast of Algeria, he insisted that he did not read Camus for his ideas.[21] While the essays he admired, 'Summer in Algiers' and others, had appeared in French in an early collection, *Noces*, they appeared in English only in 1955 together with *The Myth of Sisyphus*, Camus's earliest meditation on suicide and the Absurd. It is evident that, in later years, McGahern made 'the image' the cornerstone of his work and critical pronouncements, yet it is also evident in *The Barracks* that certain ideas and images of Camus stayed with him, and indeed particular notions expounded by Beckett in *Proust* and alluded to in a novel like *Malone Dies* also remained with him in the composition of the novel and other fiction of the 1960s. In fact, it may be that it was only in the writing of the novel, through the characterization of Elizabeth, that he was able to articulate a way of thinking that would really engage with the Nothingness and the Absurd in this post-war outlook. In this way, he may have been challenged by the existentialist orientation associated with Camus or Beckett to clarify his own thinking and his poetic method.

Many years later, in answering the question 'What is my language?', McGahern focused on what was his more lasting interest in Beckett's writing—voice, language, the difficulties of communication—and it may be that this interest was provoked right at the start by the Dublin production of *Waiting for Godot*. It is not so much that he found Beckett's language to be an Irish vernacular—something Beckett had deliberately tried to avoid in post-war work by deciding to write in French; rather, he was engaged by the 'familiar and foreign' aspects of the English language as spoken in Ireland, something Joyce had also noted. Joyce had situated a certain alienation of speaker from medium in the context of the overshadowing presence of the displaced Gaelic, but McGahern's context is different: 'In Beckett, language itself is a character and a presence, comically and sometimes even tragically aware of itself', and he highlights a feature of Beckett's style: 'the awareness of nuance so intense that the words seem to be turning in on themselves'. Linking Beckett with Bergson and Pirandello, McGahern remarks on 'a difficulty beyond language, where silence becomes a part of speech'.[22] While he goes on to refer to the Gaelic/English context in considering the Irish vernacular, something he had a very finely tuned ear for later in the dialogue of his characters, it is more likely that at this time *Waiting for Godot* opened up to him a stylistic and philosophical world associated with post-war Paris. The late remarks on Beckett situate his interest in silence and speech, the isolation of the inner self and the difficulties of communicating, and the self-consciousness of the artist working with language and received literary genres—all topics that will engage McGahern over many decades as a writer. But, to begin with, the Paris-based author of this startling and enigmatic play must have aroused his interest in an Irishman who had suddenly emerged as an acclaimed successor to Joyce.

4

'Writing all the time'

It is impossible to establish quite when McGahern's 'secret vocation' changed from aspiration to action, to the drafting of fictional episodes, since it was only in 1959 that he began to reveal the fiction he was working on even to close friends. It is likely that as soon as he settled into Clontarf in September 1956, he adopted the routine of writing every afternoon once the children left for home. There is reason to believe that he may have started earlier, but it does seem that for a time he may have devoted his energy to writing poetry rather than prose, or as well as prose. In July 1958, for instance, he enclosed three poems in a letter to Tony Whelan: 'I picked these poems for you from nine or ten that I attempted since Christmas. I have no opinion on them. I wouldn't send them anywhere—I would be getting them back, you see! I would like to believe they are not without merit'.[1] In any event, the manuscripts from the 1950s which survive in the archive in the National University of Ireland, Galway, do not tell the whole story, nor are they in chronological order. Indeed, it is a little mystery as to why these particular manuscripts survived and not others. Nevertheless, from what has survived, it is possible to draw some conclusions about McGahern's earliest impulses as a writer of fiction.

The apprentice work of the 1950s reveals in the same way as *Memoir* does, written more than forty years later, that much of McGahern's fiction is grounded in the material given to him by his own experience, and confirms that the redemption of the personal life is central to his whole work. 'As long as you believe in yourself nothing can happen to you', he wrote to Tony Whelan, enclosing the poems. 'Your proper books must be your life, to shape experience, to be able to leave life with some grace.' Even though he always offered guarded comments on the autobiographical basis of fiction, and said his greatest mistakes were made when he stayed too close to the autobiographical, this is still true, most of all in his many efforts to dramatize the experience of the dying mother and the adolescence with a brutal father. Remarkably, in one manuscript draft, the character of the dying mother is referred to as 'Susan', the young boy at her deathbed as 'John', and there are other signs that he always stayed very close to what he knew intimately and recalled vividly. The emergence of the writing self from the autobiographical experience is the life-blood of the whole achievement. In this sense, it is striking that in *The Dark* young Mahoney singles out from the priest's bookcase Tolstoy's *Resurrection*. The theme of the novel is personal redemption, and the novelist has a character remark: 'As some author once said, we also "write with our heart's blood".' It appears that the author in question is, in fact, Tolstoy himself, and McGahern's awareness of this remark is confirmed in *The Pornographer* when the writer comments, 'Nothing ever holds together unless it is mixed with some of one's own blood.'[2] There is little doubt that the talent in McGahern's fiction is revealed in the quality of the language and the elaboration of style more than in the invention of plots, characters, and settings; these elements of fiction were borrowed from personal experience because McGahern's overriding need was to discover meaning in the unique images that arose from his own circumstances.

But it is not in a literal sense of transcription, reportage, or exposé that the autobiographical issue is central. It is in the Yeatsian sense that poetry is made from the quarrel with oneself. From the earliest stages, McGahern's ambition was high and he knew that his own experience would be the quarry for his fiction. The Yeatsian lines were certainly known to him: 'The rhetorician would deceive his neighbours, / The sentimentalist himself; while art / Is but a vision of reality.'[3] It is clear that McGahern studiously avoided the quarrel with others that resulted in rhetoric, that his chosen material was primarily private, and the danger and the difficulty he had to struggle against was sentimentality, or, in other words, 'self-expression'. He struggled against allowing special privilege to the individual self, just as much as he accepted that art had to be created from the deepest knowledge, the most profound feelings, of that self.

His lifelong aversion to self-expression can be understood by way of Proust's remark in one of his favourite essays: 'For if the words we use are chosen, not by what is deepest in our thought, but by a desire to paint our own portrait, they end by expressing only that desire and not ourselves at all.'⁴ And, so, it is not altogether surprising that McGahern's first and longest battle with himself is in the search for the appropriate way to dramatize the impact on him of his mother's death and his bewildered adolescent state in the barracks in Coote-hall. To begin with, that battle was focused on a story called 'The Going'. He sent a late version of an account of a boy visiting his mother's deathbed to the *New Yorker* in February 1963 with the comment: 'I enclose a story that I have been working on and giving up for a very long time, trying to find shape for the personal experience out of which it began.'⁵ An earlier version had become the opening chapter of 'The End or the Beginning of Love', and the episode was later incorporated into *The Leavetaking* and, later still, in *Memoir*. But a lesser battle, and one he abandoned, saving only a scene for a short story, focused on his experience in London in the summer of 1954.

The untitled manuscript, certainly one of McGahern's first at-tempts to write an extended fiction, is set in London and uses emi-grant experience to investigate some characteristic McGahern themes: displacement and alienation, faith, uncertainty, and existen-tial choice. It is a novella-length draft and appears to have been written before he embarked on the autobiographical novel 'The End or the Beginning of Love'. The characterization lacks depth, the realization of the setting is thin, but there are extraordinary pas-sages of good writing, and it is unmistakably the work of McGahern. The protagonist, a young man who travels to London and works on a building site with Irish emigrants, is named Jude, presumably after the patron saint of hopeless cases (oddly, this was the given name of his brother, who became Frank at the age of six). This name for his alter ego is not the only example of a black humour that surfaces from time to time in the narrative. While it is not possible to know how closely the events of the story reflect actual experiences, there can be little doubt that the reaction of the young man to what he observes in London and his intellectual evolution there, especially in relation to his religious faith, closely mirror McGahern's state at that time or shortly thereafter when he came to write.

It is interesting that he should choose to set this early fiction in London, away from the landscape he knew best and from the family material that would become his central preoccupation for much of his career. It foreshadows the significant place London will have in much of the later fiction, and it may be that it was written in an attempt to actually discover what he felt during this time in London, to dramatize his state of mind and to situate it intellectually. It is a straightforward narrative of a young man travelling outside his provincial Irish environment and undergoing a test of his cultural formation. The investigation of the young man's character in the events that are dramatized reveals a remarkable clarity of conception and detachment in the objectification of recent experience. At certain moments, it is possible to hear one of the voices that recurred in the fiction of the early decades, a disaffected, somewhat cynical and despairing voice, but it is less honed than in, say, many of the stories of *Nightlines* or in the concluding chapter of *The Dark*. The ambition may be to use emigrant Irish experience to write an international fiction with a disaffected protagonist.

The novella opens with the night crossing on the emigrant boat to Holyhead and situates the protagonist quickly in this environment of displacement and transition. ' "Do you belong to these people?", Jude asked himself. "You have no need to go. These people must go because they have to work. They are the ignorant and the unlucky. These are representatives of Ireland's vast spiritual empire", he thought, and wished for the sanity of laughter, but it broke sickeningly within him.'[6] Initially detached, isolated, intellectually superior to the others on this 'cattle-boat', he will know them better, and himself too, by the end of the novella.

In fact, during his first meeting with his sister in London—named Rosaleen in the fiction, as in life—the complexity of the uprooted state is set out. Here are the different reasons for emigrating, overlapping with the contradictory emotions and judgements:

'Most of the Irish over here are the lowest of the low; they're the dregs of the country. You'd be ashamed of them; you don't know what they are like', Rosaleen said.

'Well, aren't we part of them now?'

'No, no', she said fiercely.

'There's no shopkeeper's brat pulling at your breasts! You're able
to throw your father's letters into the fire. It gave you freedom', he
said.

She began to weep silently.

Unlike his sister, the young man is able to gain distance from feeling
through a willed detachment. As suggested by *The Dark* and *Memoir*,
this psychological condition reflects McGahern's own state from
mid-adolescence (practised in his dealings with his father), but there
may be more to it. There is a clear determination to free himself in
an almost existentialist manner: 'His mind seemed to have forgotten
this past and his future, and to linger caressingly over every undula-
tion of the bus, the sunlight on the blue petrol fumes, in the warm
sensual glow of the living moment. Tomorrow he was beginning a
new life. Was he not beginning it now? Ireland a green map came
into his mind but he thrust it impatiently away.' At any rate, the
early 'freedom' he enjoys and the belief that he can begin 'a new
life' so easily are quickly dispelled when he is faced with the reality
of finding a job.

Dismissed by the clerk in the labour exchange in a manner that
betrays racist contempt, he begins to come down to earth, and,
through the good luck of living with his former school friend
Campbell—one of those who had to emigrate—he is put in touch
with an Irishman who will hire him for manual labour on a building site. The circumstances of the workplace are depicted in great
detail, the physically exhausting work itself, and the different men
who work there. The reality of how all of them have been transformed by their circumstances is vividly revealed. Much of the
detail here reappears in 1968 in the snapshot version of this
experience, 'Hearts of Oak and Bellies of Brass': the various characters with their county names, such as 'Tipperary', the marginalized Jocko who makes his way onto the site only to be sprayed
with liquid concrete, and even the refrain: 'Shite or twist, shovel
or burst'.

'Hearts of Oak, Bellies of Brass' preserves the rough and crude
way of life of the emigrants; they are revealed in their context without commentary or judgement. In the draft novella, however, since
the characterization of Jude is central, his revulsion and his rever-
sion to attitudes of his past are made clear:

In all the speech about him obscenities and blasphemies were used as commands and greetings: language without the violence of the blasphemous or obscene seemed to have no meaning for them. Its coarseness grated on him, but was this loud vulgarity worse than the mannish jokes and timorous blasphemies of the college students. Was it not its logical conclusion? These people had no sense of sin; the levity with which they handled the Holy Name and sex almost terrified him; he almost expected the wrath of God would come like thunder and lightning to blacken this city off the face of the earth, this huge Sodom of the restless earth.

In fact, while considerable attention is given to this emigrant world, it is the moral and religious struggle of the alienated protagonist that emerges as the primary preoccupation.

Jude lives with his friend Campbell, who has been in London already for some considerable time. He has abandoned Catholicism, and Jude's inner struggle with the issue of faith is counterpointed with Campbell's apparent disinterest:

[Jude] had drifted into neglect: he hadn't gone to Mass. He had put Mary [apparently, his devout girlfriend back in Ireland] out of his mind, but now when he had become accustomed to the work, the anguish of faith renewed itself. Some force seemed to drag him out of the rooms towards the nearby church of St. Ann's...He saw his right hand unconsciously rise to his forehead to begin the sign of the Cross as if at the beginning or end of a prayer or sacrifice...It beat in his brain like a tribal dance.

While this atavistic emotion seems programmed, and he is critical of his loss of the ability to decide for himself ('some force', 'tribal dance'), the compromise he works out takes into account the ineradicable, unconscious stirrings of his earliest formation:

He had a puritan's pessimistic dissatisfaction with life, the rich imaginative power of his race, and the unconscious willingness to make himself the arena of conflict for the two. While he fulfilled the bare skeleton of his religious duties he could be at peace; but to stay away was to stir until it seethed the inhuman hell of his imagination. Reason was of no avail: the stronger he fought it twice stronger it grew, until almost by a madness of torture he was forced into the outward acceptance of Ritual. In the simple observance of his religious duties he did not hope to avoid hell but to quiet the hell of his imagination.

This is a distinctly pragmatic resolution of the question of faith or religious practice, 'to quiet the hell of his imagination', but it shows a shrewd and eloquent insight on McGahern's part into the troubled state of the young man.

The plotting of the novel in its later stages shows the success of the two friends in finding girlfriends. The couples go out to dancehalls and bars and appear to be launched into an adult life that will integrate them into the society about them. After some months, Jude breaks off his relationship with Ann, but Campbell decides to stay with Irene and they make plans to marry. One day, following a romantic evening during which Campbell and Irene win the spot prize at a dance, Campbell is killed in an accident on the building site. The event comes without warning, and appears to be the same incident as is presented later in the story 'Faith, Hope and Charity'. But the contexts given to the incident in the two fictions are remarkably different. Jude is unable to comfort the distraught Irene; in fact, he treats her rather coldly, protecting himself from the devastation of his own raw feelings. And at the graveside, his struggle with faith seems to reach a resolution: 'Habit can enforce social and religious ritual long after the rites themselves have ceased either to have vitality or meaning. Jude turned away from the ceremony at the graveside almost unafraid: habit would no longer draw him back to the rites without meaning: he was free.' The price for this freedom from old feelings and interpretations appears to be a bleak and isolated detachment.

Yet this unexpectedly brutal end to a fiction of growth is surely characteristic of a certain aspect of McGahern's later vision. The future is never a given, nor must it be taken for granted, even in romantic or liberated circumstances, and childhood's end is inevitable, leaving the adult with the burden of searching for an authentic vision of life. Given these facts of life, the quest for purpose, belief, or morality must be consciously undertaken, and this early fiction shares with *The Barracks* and *The Dark* that very serious outlook. In fact, it may be that the crucially important events in *The Barracks*—the love affair in London with Halliday, and his sudden death—are a development of this scene of Campbell's death. While Elizabeth moves past that event in facing her own death and coming to terms with it, this fiction of a young man ends with a brief scene of black comedy. Sligo, another one of the Irish labourers, who may replace Campbell in the flat, goes

drinking with Jude, and the pair make their way down the street sing-
ing Percy French's well-known air 'The Mountains of Mourne': '"And
others are diggin' for gold in the streets", he sang, ending in an outrageous cackle of laughter.' This concluding line surely foreshadows
lines in the final chapter of *The Dark*: 'It seemed that the whole world
must turn over in the night and howl in its boredom, for the father
and for the son and for the whole shoot, but it did not.'[7]

Whenever this fiction was written, sometime in the mid-1950s,
most likely, it is a clear indication that the young McGahern found
material in this summer of 1954 that would be of major significance
in his body of fiction and, related to that material, the beginning of
a narrative voice. The London experience, or, more generally, the
adult urban experience of the Dublin years, focused in more impersonal ways the philosophical and cultural issues implicit in his childhood and youth, and these became part of the material he would
have to digest. Writing to Tony Whelan, who is now back in London,
he appears to already know the core conviction of his work: 'But it
hardly matters where you are! Suffering cannot be better developed
in one part of the world than another...London may be the meet-
ing-place of the world; it seems to me that the meetings are no different in London than in Cootehall.'[8] In the decision to abandon
this 'London' fiction, the direction that McGahern will follow triumphantly in *The Barracks* and *The Dark* and in later work can be clearly
foreseen. He revealed his uncertainty to Tony Whelan, and his bitterness, his disillusionment with teaching, his wish to travel, his
loneliness—'No one seems to even know about literature anymore;
to realize death'—but the maturity of his thinking and writing are
already remarkable in a young man not yet twenty-four.

5

'Art is solitary man'

Established in Dublin, McGahern entered into what he called 'a Freemasonry of the intellect with a vigorous underground life of its own that paid scant regard to Church or State'. He refers to the 'clownish system', the 'paternalistic mishmash' that he was obliged to subscribe to in his daily duties: 'the system was so blatantly foolish in so many of its manifestations that it could only provoke the defence of laughter, though never, then, in public'. That freemasonry, glimpsed in the friendships with Jimmy Swift and Kavanagh's entourage, perhaps too with some of his new colleagues at Belgrove School, he later presented in a somewhat urbane way. 'People who need to read, who need to think and see, will always find a way round a foolish system, and difficulty will only make that instinct stronger, as it serves in another sphere to increase desire.'[1] Frustration and desire: the sexual analogy surely suggests that the later urbanity masks a visceral struggle, as does the expression 'paternalistic mishmash', which recalls his own father's regime in the barracks.

The urge to subvert and oppose was sharpened in this freemasonry, but the ease with which the process is described in later years passes over the major work of self-mastery and self-management that would allow talent to bloom in such repressive circumstances. He speaks of their Flaubertian view on freedom of expression: 'even an obscene book, we would argue, could not be immoral if it was truly written'. They believed they could write 'in complete freedom' and thought little of censorship or of the absurd aspects of the institutions in which they had to work. Any banned books worth reading 'could be easily found and quickly passed around', so that in no way did they feel cut off from ideas or literature they might wish to read. Yet it is clear that in spite of such casual remarks there was an inevitable strain, the strain of opposition, the constant double life of social circumstances, the obligation to be truthful in a context of half-truths and fantasies. Anyone who aspired to write well had to be vigilant not only towards the sham and posturing of the surrounding society but towards the world of the arts too: 'This climate also served to cut out a lot of the pious humbug that often afflicts the arts.' If one version of this underground community speaks of it as enabling, such remarks hint that all was not so easy for a young writer whose deepest need was to recognize and articulate 'true thought and true feeling'.

The harshness of some sentences about the Kavanagh coterie in *Memoir* suggests that there was no ease of passage for the young McGahern, although he continued to have occasional contacts with them in the years ahead. He speaks with distaste of the 'bohemian bars' around Grafton Street: 'Like all closed, self-protective societies, they believed that everything of importance took place within their circle, while all of them were looking outwards without seeing in this any contradiction.'[2] The freemasonry had its limitations and its dangers for one who valued his independence more than anything else. That independence had been hard won, and there is a clear suggestion in *Memoir* that, fifty years before, the lesson he had learned in his father's house was relevant in literary circles too: 'The violence and megalomania and darkness of these bars were as familiar to me as the air around my father.' Clearly, Kavanagh was a 'father-figure' for this literary set. McGahern kept his distance, from the personal 'megalomania and darkness' as well as from literary politics and territories, although how soon he clarified all this to himself is uncertain. The personal strain of preserving independence, while at the same time drawing support from the knowledge that Kavanagh was a very talented poet, underlies these remarks.

'The minute the writer takes up a pen', he often quoted Chekhov, 'he accuses himself of unanswerable egotism and all he can do with any decency after that is to bow.'[3] For years he will rely on this principle as the reason for self-deprecation and silence: 'Chekhov's words were one of our early texts in the "good manners" of the mind.' 'Egotism' and 'good manners' mark the exigent personal struggle he will be undertaking in the years ahead. It is unclear who 'our' refers to in this sentence, but it may not be living people around Dublin, for he is echoing Proust, who wrote in 'Days of Reading':

> If, the more intelligent a man is, the greater is his taste for reading, so, too, as we have seen, is he less exposed to its dangers. An original mind can subordinate its reading to its own personal activity. For its owner it is no more than the noblest of distractions, and the most ennobling too, for reading and knowledge are alone capable of teaching 'good manners' to the mind. The power of sensibility and intelligence can be developed only in ourselves, in the depths of our spiritual life.[4]

More than anything else, this passage tells what McGahern was about in these few years at the end of the 1950s.

When he looked back and spoke of a freemasonry, he was really remembering Proust, who completed this paragraph in which he defines the 'good manners' of the mind: 'In the world of thinkers, as in the world of society, there is such a thing as distinction, as nobility, as a sort of freemasonry of mental habits and a heritage of traditions.' And a few sentences before, in this essay that McGahern will know well before the end of the 1950s, Proust wrote of books as a 'mirror' of personality, one further example of how intimately McGahern's critical vocabulary and beliefs are borrowed from Proust. In his last decades, such terms and many others became habitual, almost all of them discovered in the 1950s in his own learning of the good manners of the mind. The more important freemasonry that McGahern joined, then, was that set of classic writers whom he discovered and made his own in the years between 1956 and 1959, the writers and their traditions that became 'mirrors' for himself, pre-eminent among them Yeats and Proust.

'The knowledge of reality is always in some measure a secret knowledge; it is a kind of death.'[5] McGahern quoted this line from Yeats's *Autobiographies* to characterize this phase of his development and to signal the central importance of Yeats to it. He went on to comment that this was 'socially as well as metaphorically true'.[6] It is a puzzling, retrospective statement, as if he wants to suggest that the 'secret' knowledge he coveted alienated him from the society of other people: 'it is a kind of death'. What he discovered was something he could not share with other people, perhaps, or that 'the knowledge of reality' made relationships difficult. He seems to suggest that he became alienated from human intercourse, or, simply, guarded about what he knew, even in discovering the truth about human nature. 'Humankind cannot bear very much reality' is not a statement of Yeats but of T. S. Eliot, another significant figure in McGahern's freemasonry. Yet, whatever the social cost, there is no doubt that it was that very 'knowledge of reality' which he made his goal in these years.

It is clear that McGahern's interest in Yeats moved from the poet of Sligo, of knowable places, of beautiful lines resonating with untranslatable symbols, to the life of the poet himself, or at least to his autobiographical writings. The timing of the publication of *Autobiographies* in 1955 is surely right for the young McGahern to take notice. The knowledge he seeks is knowledge of oneself, and so the memoirs, letters, and biographies of artists will constitute a body of texts in which he will come upon 'mirrors' of his own emerging identity. Among many such artists whom he investigated in this way, Yeats was the first. McGahern said that the poet was the first writer with whom he experienced the sense of mirroring which converted him into a 'moral' reader and that he returned more often to Yeats's work than to any other writer's because it gave him more pleasure. This pleasure in reading and rereading, a primary criterion of critical judgement for McGahern, is attributable not only to the intimate eloquence of the style; Yeats's conviction and confidence as a poet can be felt in his style and their origins observed in his larger body of work, autobiographical and critical.

What was this intimate knowledge and pleasure he found in contemplating the image of Yeats's life and work? The simple answer seems to be the one given in *The Leavetaking* and already referred to. When Patrick Moran's mother explains to the nun in her classroom why she writes a poem on the blackboard for the children to memorize, she expresses a simple faith in poetry as an artistic medium: 'It can be felt but not known, as we can never know our own life or another's in the great mystery of life itself.'[7] This is a paradoxical kind of knowledge founded on what cannot be known, on mystery, a knowledge that can be felt, although not everyone may wish to feel it. In a surprising twist, this teacher/mother of Patrick Moran, himself a teacher, had learned 'that most teachers read little, had even an instinctive hatred of the essential magic and mystery in all real poetry, reducing it to the factual or sentimental or preferably both'. She goes on to give a line from Yeats, 'The wet winds blow out of the clinging air', as an example of the 'magical twist' that transforms ordinary expression into poetry, 'the infusion of the poetical personality into the words'. The simple answer is, then, that McGahern felt that Yeats wrote 'real poetry', and what this means is that the poet creates a style of images and symbols, of rhythm and form, of dialogue and drama which embodies his deepest feeling and clearest thinking about the nature of reality.

An essay by Yeats, 'The Symbolism of Poetry', lies behind this passage in *The Leavetaking*, but McGahern does not admire Yeats primarily for his intellect, his ideas, or his philosophies; he admires the 'magic and mystery' of his 'poetical personality', his way of being a poet in the world. In other words, he admired the accomplishment and power of the poetry itself, of particular poems. He memorized them. He had an extensive repertoire of poems, many lines from which are echoed in the textures of his own literary speech. Over and above favourite lines and poems was the character of Yeats as poet. He was 'a very great poet' who possessed a 'secret knowledge' which was embodied in his poetry, and when McGahern spoke of his own 'secret vocation', it is evident that he is speaking of something not really communicable to even his literary friends; the mother in *The Leavetaking* needed to protect herself from ridicule for her love of poetry, and so she belonged 'in a secret society of one'. Reader and poet are both solitary. It is very likely that, beneath the eloquent and beautiful language of Yeats, McGahern felt a man who suffered, who was haunted by death and craved eternal life. Yeats's constant explorations in religions and Neoplatonic systems of thought were fuelled by a desolate sense of 'whatever is begotten, born and dies', and from his search he brought back images for poetry. McGahern had little interest in the spiritualistic Yeats, or the folkloric Yeats, or the cultural nationalist, or the philosopher of history, but he was most certainly moved by his images.

He was first drawn to Yeats's work by the knowledge of reality in these early poems of Sligo. The feelings of young love, of dream, and disappointment found their objective correlative in local place names, and in a landscape that McGahern could recognize. His English teacher at St Pat's, Jim Rigney, a Sligoman, had a personal attachment to Yeats's work and spoke of it to the students—this, perhaps, being the only formal study of literature at the institution which affected McGahern. Reading *Autobiographies* and the *Essays and Introductions* later, he found a whole personality articulated, with a sense of the poet as maker of his own spiritual life, as it were, and with a sense of tradition as an inspiring presence. Yeats's search for Unity of Being was revealed to him, and while Yeats exemplified the poet's magisterial sense of selfhood, he also exemplified that work of making, and the risks of that 'fascination of what's difficult'. The vocation of poet demands an integration of a wide range of feelings and also an unceasing labour: 'He is of all things not impossible the most difficult, for that only which comes easily can never be a portion of our being.'[8] These words, echoed in McGahern, appear in a chapter called 'Anima Hominis' of a small book *Per Amica Silentia Lunae*, reprinted in *Mythologies*; so many echoes from this essay appear in McGahern's own prose that it is clear that he had sought it out and was deeply affected by it.

Yeats's prose writings reveal the range and depth of his reflection on literary figures and traditions, Irish, English, French, ancient Greek, and Gaelic, in translation, and, significantly, from an early age, he benefited from a father who was singularly devoted to the artistic life, to knowing artists as well as paintings and books. In the part of *Autobiographies* called 'Reveries over Childhood and Youth', McGahern found an achronological narrative of images from Yeats's childhood in Sligo, which to a degree anticipates his own method in the early part of *Memoir*, but he may have been struck most of all in that book by the characterization of Yeats's father, the painter John Butler Yeats:

He did not care even for a fine lyric passage unless he felt some actual man behind its elaboration of beauty, and he was always looking for the lineaments of some desirable, familiar life...All must be an idealization of speech, and at some moment of passionate action or somnambulistic reverie...He despised the formal beauty of Raphael, that calm which is not an ordered passion but an hypocrisy, and attacked Raphael's

life for its love of pleasure and its self-indulgence…He no
longer read me anything for its story, and all our discussion
was of style.[9]

So many of these convictions of the father will become convictions
of the son and, in time, of McGahern also, and many of his repeated dicta can be traced back to Yeats and to Yeats's father. But
he would probably never have trusted these dicta, or borrowed a
critical and intellectual framework from them, if he had not first
found an intimate pleasure and exhilaration in the style of the great
poems. Their presence can be felt in many of McGahern's later
stories and novels.[10]

'J.B.Y. was a well-remembered presence in Dublin when I was
young, sometimes referred to affectionately as "the old man who ran
away from home and made good".'[11] This is a reference to the fact
that when Yeats's father went on a visit to New York in late 1907
he never returned, and the new life he found in exile was not only
satisfactory to the restless and unsuccessful portrait painter but it
created the occasion over almost fifteen years for his lasting literary
legacy: the extraordinary letters written mostly to W.B. Almost fifty
years later, McGahern recalls this time in Dublin in the Introduction he wrote to a selection of John Butler Yeats's letters: 'There
were still people alive then who could recall his brilliant conversation. Occasionally fragments of his speech could be heard quoted,
one of which—"Those people who complain about Willie's high
style should remember that when he sits down to write his verses
Willie always puts on his top hat"—I have never been able to discover anywhere in print.' These remarks reveal McGahern's affection for Yeats *père*, or at least for the image of the man created by
recollections, by his son's evocation of him in 'Reveries over Childhood and Youth', and by the celebrated letters. Ezra Pound edited
a small selection of excerpts in 1917, and other selections appeared
before McGahern prepared his edition, but this was a labour of
honouring a historical figure who had become real to him in the
1950s and of personal significance.

The letters are a continuation of the 'brilliant conversation', and
McGahern seems to draw close to the writer in saying that 'J.B.Y.
loved letters. Along with the works of Shakespeare and Montaigne,

the letters of Lamb and Keats were always by his side during the New York years.' The essence of the man was equally expressed in the unrecorded conversation and, while it is clear that McGahern agrees with Yeats's characterization of the artistic life, he also values the fact that his beliefs are embodied in his behaviour; unlike his son, he did not work incessantly to perfect his art. 'I suspect that, like most of his life, [the remark recalled earlier] was scattered with an open hand on to the living air, no thought being given to its furtherance or preservation until it was articulated again as a new, exciting fresh thought.' While the father and son may be seen as 'last Romantics' in many of their beliefs regarding the character of the poet, McGahern repeatedly draws attention to the absence of egotism in the character of the father. 'At that time, while his admired portraits hung in the National and Municipal Galleries and the marvellous letters could be found in libraries and rare bookshops, it was thought that his genius was something more than he had ever managed to get down on canvas or in print. He can never be accused of that exhibitionism when the means of expression is in excess of what is being said.' In other words, McGahern saw Yeats as an unappreciated genius because he did not accomplish what others believed he should have, whereas, more significantly, he did accomplish what was exactly in keeping with his own nature. The occasional letters were a literary genre revealing a depth of feeling and clarity of thinking which any literary genre must possess; for McGahern, Yeats *père* exemplified a minor and yet pure form of artistic authenticity.

In an extraordinary passage in one of the letters, this man of Protestant background appears to characterize himself, Shakespeare, and all true artists as 'Catholic Agnostics':

> Catholic Agnosticism is full of self-knowledge, self-esteem, it makes people reason with themselves rather than with other people, the result of this spirit are humility and sympathy, and much probing of the soul of man. Protestant Agnosticism makes a man turn his eyes outward, to watch the doings of other people, and when it reasons it does so contentiously in hot debate with other disputants.[12]

In this odd distinction, an idea elaborated in New York in 1914 is rehearsed:

The emphasis of the orator and the teacher bears no relation to the emphasis of the poet—indeed is fatal to it... *Art is solitary man*, the man as he is behind the innermost, the utmost veils. That is why with the true poet we do not care what are his persuasions, opinions, ideas, religion, moralities—through all these we can pierce to the voice of the essential man if we have the discerning senses.[13]

In such formulations, the impassioned older man seeks to guide his son, to urge him to keep to the poet's path, or simply to express his own faith in 'personality' rather than 'character', or in the 'vision of reality' which the poet will soon thereafter declare is the poet's business, a poetry that does not yield to either rhetoric or sentimentality. The intimate relationship of father and son, grounded finally on the recognition of style as the essential self of the artist, appears to have been deeply moving to McGahern, and he frequently returns to these key ideas in later years as an anchor of personal conviction.

Central to McGahern's outlook from now on was that poetry and literary prose must achieve Yeats's ideal: 'the calm that is an ordered passion'. The passage regarding the father from *Autobiographies* puts it most succinctly and in a form often quoted by McGahern. And along with that is a further dictum from *Autobiographies*: 'The self-conquest of the writer who is not a man of action is style' and Yeats associates style with 'the moral element', as would McGahern later.[14] The 'ordered passion' that is art is a simple formula for almost any emotion that has to be conquered, whether love or fear or despair, but it is evident in Yeats that suffering is the experience that needs most pressingly to find a calm expression. Yeats's ideas on tragedy, especially in relation to Synge's life and work, would certainly have struck a chord also. And so it is possible to detect the reasons why McGahern would remain attached to the Yeatses, *père et fils*, all his life for here he found the idea of the self-conquest of literary creation and in Yeats's poetry the fruit of that self-conquest.

He did not go on to become a poet, but as a writer he assumed the character of the poet, and there is no doubt that what he learned of the poet's character from his reading of Yeats lies beneath his career in writing fiction.

Admiration of Yeats was wholehearted and clearly articulated, all through his life, but his attitude to the other inescapable figure in Irish writing is somewhat ambivalent. 'I admire Joyce, but I don't feel very close to him', he remarked late in life. In explanation, he contrasted Joyce and Yeats: 'For instance nearly all of Joyce's wit is aural, it is of the ear, while I think Yeats has always interested me more in a sense because I think I see things with the eyes, much better. I have no criticism. I think Joyce is a great writer.'[15] It is a distinction repeated elsewhere, but it is hardly sustained by a consideration of McGahern's debt to the two writers, for while it is true that he is much preoccupied with 'seeing', his language draws on powerful aural elements, as in Joyce's early work, and indeed on aural elements in the poetry of Yeats also. His loyalty to Yeats seems to have come first and was in some sense fundamental: 'It is difficult to imagine Joyce and Beckett without Yeats.' Another comment may be a clue to the question of loyalty: 'I did object very much to the Romantic notion of the artist, you know that was cultivated by Joyce, when I was young. I actually resented the notion of the artist as hero, and I saw it—I still see it basically as a sort of nineteenth century sentimentality.'[16] In this regard, it is difficult to separate Joyce from Yeats, for the poet was surely as committed to the 'artist as hero' as Joyce may be said to have been. In fact, the 'sentimentality' may have more to do with the Joycean self-portrait depicted in Stephen Dedalus, and more generally, the portrayal of the urban Catholic intellectual in *A Portrait of the Artist as a Young Man*, for there is a striking absence of self-effacement or humility in the self-dramatizations of the young Joyce as he went into exile. The autobiographical basis of Joyce's characterization of Dedalus and the claim to privilege as an artist or thinker may have been temperamentally difficult for McGahern to associate with, but there is no doubt that, as the most important writer of prose fiction in Ireland, Joyce was a member of the 'freemasonry' and his work another 'mirror' for the young McGahern.

He mentions that he first heard of Joyce's work from Éanna Ó hEither in St Pat's, but very soon he would learn of how important Joyce was to Patrick Kavanagh and the Swifts, and of Joyce's international reputation. A friend reports a conversation with him in the mid-1950s: 'I remember an evening in his flat when we discussed

James Joyce, particularly the short stories in *Dubliners*. I had read them quickly one after the other without digesting them too much whereas he talked with insight and enthusiasm about his favourite, "The Dead".[17] That enthusiasm is evident in a letter to Michael McLaverty in 1959. Much later, he will remark:

> It was a long journey: from the scrupulous clarity of *Dubliners*, where the first shapes are, where the wonderful aural wit first stirs, crux upon crux—out into *Finnegans Wake*, the words now losing their definite line to merge and chime and swim, calling up other words, always changing, always taling, summoned up by the incredible energy of that comic genius, always expanding, expounding, playing. Words alone seem certain good. Talk will save us. We have left the world of letters and reached impure ground.[18]

Perhaps most tellingly, then, the increasingly experimental stylistic and linguistic features of Joyce's later work appeared to McGahern to be intellectually controlled and lacking in vitality. In late 1961, he wrote to John Montague with regard to *The Barracks* which he had begun a few months earlier: 'I think what you say of the need for structure true, but I think it must be *unique* or organic, growing out of the struggle with the material, and not a superimposed structure as in Joyce and Eliot. No matter how great that achievement, it ends in academic sterility, and I think our generation must move in the opposite direction—to survive and grow.'[19] There may have been a certain rivalry, an intergenerational rivalry often observed in literary history, or indeed an 'anxiety of influence', which made him hesitant to adopt a method or an aesthetic approach, yet in spite of the hesitation or distance he kept between himself and Joyce he knew that he and Joyce belonged in a similar tradition.

In his essay on *Dubliners* of twenty-five years later, one can detect the outline of his reading of that tradition. He contrasts Joyce with George Moore and Kavanagh, writers in a mode of 'rampant individualism and localism', whereas 'Joyce's temperament was essentially classical, and he knew exactly what he was attempting in *Dubliners*.'[20] He was a more conscious artist, then, and McGahern clearly admires the 'authority and plain sense' shown in a letter about his plan for *Dubliners*: Joyce 'was well aware that he was working within a clearly defined tradition...In *Dubliners*, there is no self-expression; its truth is in every phrase. "The author is like God in nature, present everywhere but nowhere visible."' McGahern certainly subscribed to this impersonality of style, the conscious art that arises from an awareness of the freemasonry of French literary tradition. 'The method in *Dubliners* is that people, events, and places invariably find their true expression',[21] and even if it is difficult to argue that the appreciation he expressed in the 1980s was something he felt in the late 1950s, there are signs that he did appreciate Joyce's method and the original inspiration that arose from his own self and his immediate surroundings.

McGahern spends much of his essay outlining his understanding of the tradition to which Joyce belonged, and there can be little doubt that from *The Barracks* on he situated himself in this tradition. It is the French prose tradition which comes down from Flaubert, and McGahern's strategy is to allow Flaubert to state his own principles and method by quoting from his correspondence with George Sand in 1876 and from a report by Henry James on a soirée at Flaubert's Paris apartment: 'art and morality are two perfectly different things...The only duty of a novel was to be well-written; that merit included every other of which it is capable.'[22] These words of James, summarizing the dominant beliefs of Flaubert and his circle, are echoed down through McGahern's career, just as Flaubert's pithy remark about the invisible artist like God in nature is quoted by Joyce in his letter on *Dubliners* and becomes a commonplace in McGahern's criticism, even to the point of describing Tomás Ó Criomhthain's style in *An tOileanach/ The Islandman* in just these words. In a letter to Sand, Flaubert insists on the necessary impersonality of his style whether what is depicted is ugly or beautiful: 'For the moment a thing is True, it is good. Even obscene books are immoral only if they lack truth.'[23] They are the very words of McGahern in describing the dominant view of his friends in Dublin regarding censorship.

It is evident then that Flaubert's 'classical' ideas are those of McGahern and that the work of the early Joyce, which he was able to assimilate to that tradition, greatly appealed to him. 'Its classical balance allows no room for self-expression', he wrote of *Dubliners*. When he praised the stories—'The rich local humour is never

allowed to stray out of character. It generally consists of badly digested scraps of misinformation which are adhered to like articles of
faith once they are possessed, and used like weapons to advance
their owner's sense of self-importance, or to belabour that of
others'[24]—he is providing a precise description of his own method
in dramatizing the guards in *The Barracks*.

McGahern had a regret, it seems, that only in a part of *Ulysses* did
Joyce's 'imagination return... to his first characters, his original material'. There may be an implication here that the reason he did not
warm wholeheartedly to his fellow Irishman was that Joyce had
abandoned his 'original material', and the lesson McGahern may
have drawn from the master's example was that he should stay close
to his.

In spite of what many would think of as an obsessive focus on the
details of Joyce's life—through Ellmann's biography, for instance,
which appeared to great notice in 1959—it may be that McGahern's
interest in him was also focused on the life of the artist. It appears
that his main source for this was not Ellmann but Stanislaus Joyce,
whose *My Brother's Keeper* appeared in 1958. On more than one occasion, McGahern praised Stanislaus's acute and psychologically
penetrating memoir of his brother and quoted from it. In particular,
he referred to the distinction between the romantic and classical
tempers, identifying James as embodying the latter: 'The classical
temper, he declares, accepts the place in nature that is given us
without doing violence to the gift and so fashions the events of life
that the quick intelligence can go beyond them to their meaning
which was still unuttered.'[25] In contrast, he accuses the romantic of
'creating symbols of ideals that obscure the light'. 'Radiance' derives
from the 'ecstatic contemplation' of the visible world and, in achieving that poetic intensity, 'attains to an eternal state'. Stanislaus char-
acterizes his brother as a poet, a philosopher, and a psychologist of
the given, of the laws of nature.

But Stanislaus's memoir is also notable for his insistence that
Joyce greatly admired Yeats's work, in spite of the well-known
mockery of the older artist: 'He considered him to be the greatest
poet Ireland had produced, with only Mangan worthy to be his
predecessor, and the greatest of contemporary poets.'[26] The 'sincere
homage' Joyce expressed on Yeats's death was founded on his

admiration of his poetic power and language, and he regretted that 'Yeats did not hold his head high enough for a poet of his stature.' In short, Stanislaus argues for a view of the poet's character and method which he believes both his brother and Yeats had in common, and this view of 'the poet's high office' is not, finally, so different from that of Proust.

Most strikingly, Stanislaus Joyce gave McGahern a view of Irish writing which he appears to have kept all his life:

> In Ireland, a country that has seen revolutions in every generation there is properly speaking no national tradition. Nothing is stable in the country; nothing is stable in the minds of the people. When the Irish artist begins to write, he has to create his moral world from chaos by himself, for himself... it proves to be an enormous advantage for men of original genius, such as Shaw, Yeats, or my brother.

This absence of tradition, and the moral 'chaos' which results, Stanislaus contrasts with the English tradition: 'When an English writer... deals with social, religious, or intellectual problems, one has the impression that even though the problems are real and the writer is striving to be sincere, the life that produced him is in general stable and balanced. It has been lived for centuries against a Constable background.'[27] In these words of Joyce's brother, McGahern found a way of thinking about his own situation and of Ireland which he will rely on over and over in the following decades: it might even be that in the period from *High Ground* and *Amongst Women* to *That They May Face the Rising Sun*, he set himself on a new course to imagine a sense of stability and balance in the midst of 'chaos', perhaps even to penetrate the nationalist history of revolutions in order to see Irish country life 'against a Constable background'.

Undoubtedly, the Yeatses and the Joyces were recurrently important to McGahern, and Yeats's poetry remained vital throughout his writing career. It may be, however, that Proust was more important as the one who helped him to understand the process of reading itself, as he outlined it in later decades, for in addition to Proust's novel, his essays and letters became one of his 'mirrors'. The frequency of echoes in 'The Image', his 'Prologue' to his work in 1966,

and from that point on, identify Proust as an early and lasting interpreter who links the dream-like pleasure of reading the Moroneys'
books and the 'moral activity' of this later period. McGahern came
to understand how Proust's reading in childhood, the death of his
mother, the enlargement of the spiritual life, and the refinement of
his own sensibility in full independence were integral to his years of
'training' before it became possible for him to begin to write *À la
recherche du temps perdu.*

Earlier in his life, Proust had become interested in John Ruskin's
lectures on 'How and What to Read...and Why to Read'. His impassioned preface to his translation of Ruskin's lectures opened with
the words that McGahern made his own and repeated many times:
'No days, perhaps, of all our childhood are ever so fully lived as
those that we had regarded as not lived at all: days spent wholly
with a favourite book.'[28]

Proust notes with some emphasis the difference between solitary
reading and conversations with friends, no matter how wise; nor
should reading be considered like a conversation with the authors of
classic literary work, as Ruskin had said. In this matter, McGahern
noted his agreement with Proust rather than Ruskin:

> What makes a book and a friend so different, one from an-
> other, has nothing to do with the greater or less degree of their
> wisdom, but with the manner of our communication, reading,
> as opposed to conversation, consisting, for each one of us, in
> receiving another's thought, while all the time, ourselves, re-
> maining alone, that is to say, continuing to enjoy the intel-
> lectual power which comes to us in solitude, and which
> conversation at once destroys—continuing in a state of mind
> which allows us to be inspired, to let the mind work fruitfully
> upon itself.[29]

And so, it is not so much the wisdom or the ideas contained in the
book that matter as their inspirational power in the spiritual life of
the reader. 'We can never receive the truth from anybody', Proust
writes, 'but must always be creating it for ourselves.' Solitary reading must be understood as no less than 'incitements' to a quality of
creative awakening or engagement with the essence of the author's
imaginative power: 'we want him to give us answers when all he can

offer are desires. And these desires books can awake in us only by compelling us to contemplate the final beauty to which they provide a gate.'[30] McGahern's later characterizations of his own ideal readers, free to recreate his books in their own selves, surely come back to his own experience as 'solitary reader', understood in the light of Proust's words. The creative power of the artist must evoke a similar state in the viewer or the reader, a desire that is inspiring, rather than a passive state of accepting a completed truth or a quantity of digested knowledge. 'To turn reading into a discipline is to set too great a value on what is only an initiation. It stands upon the threshold of the spirit: it can show us the way in, but it is not, in itself, that life.'[31] It is clear that the kind of reading Proust describes is not that of an academic or a critic but of a creative artist, and he repeatedly connects it with the hypnotic pleasure of childhood reading.

Unlike Proust, McGahern has left little evidence of his responses to the literature he read at this stage in his evolution, for he had no interest in being a critic or in keeping a journal. He had learned from Proust, perhaps, that while reading and writing are magically related, and writing depends on reading, it is also separate from it. Discovering oneself in the 'mirrors' that other writers hold up is key, yet preserving one's independence from the overwhelming force of the earlier writer's work is equally important, if one is to become a writer. The lessons to be learned from Proust on this subject are of significance in McGahern's 'training' for, in the end, Proust would only marginally be a model of the kind of fiction McGahern would write, yet his understanding of the artistic character is vitally present in enabling McGahern to forge and preserve a confident independence. Proust's insistence on the necessity of having one's style animated by one's own unique sensibility is forcefully affirmed and his understanding of the dangers that reading may entail for that undertaking is clear.

Proust's only concern is with the reader's 'deepest regions where the real life of the spirit has its origins'. He believes that people of powerful imagination are capable of accessing their own spiritual regions, but often, without the 'external stimulus' of great writing, 'they will end by erasing in themselves all feeling and all memory of spiritual greatness'. The 'good manners' of the mind is a matter of education in great writing, a matter of having membership in that 'freemasonry of mental habits and a heritage of traditions', and so he insists that a wide-ranging familiarity with literary traditions as well as an intensive reading of particular books are part of the necessary training.[32]

Many of the essays which illuminate Proust's own intellectual and imaginative evolution towards his great novel were collected in *Contre Sainte-Beuve*, translated by Sylvia Townsend Warner and published as *By Way of Sainte-Beuve* in 1958. McGahern said that it was one of his favourite critical books, and indeed many of his most lasting beliefs about art and the artist are articulated in it. 'That's a book of criticism that I always go back to, all the time', he said in early 1979.[33] This collection of critical writings from 1908–9 articulate Proust's own beliefs in the months when he finally realized how to launch himself into the book that he would continue to write for the rest of his life. It is likely that McGahern had read *Remembrance of Things Past* (the first English translation of *À la recherche du temps perdu*) in the mid-1950s and that he read the critical writings soon after they appeared. Certainly by early 1959 he was referring to Proust as a writer with whose work he was very familiar, and from then on, Proust stayed in his mind as a touchstone and as a shadow whose words are echoed (sometimes intentionally) in McGahern's own writing.

In Proust's essays on Flaubert and other French writers, one essay in particular stood out for McGahern: 'Chateaubriand—he's a writer I admire enormously too—I think that little essay on Chateaubriand says everything that can be said about writing.' In that essay, Proust isolates those qualities in Chateaubriand's *Mémoires d'outretombe* which make his work immortal, and in doing so, he is enabled to put behind him almost twenty years of uncertainty, false starts, and commentaries on other writers. Defining the essential poetic element to which Chateaubriand gained access, Proust defined his own essential poetry; as Proust learned from Chateaubriand, McGahern learned from Proust and discovered a sense of a literary tradition and a set of convictions about the centrality of art to his own life. For all of them, poetry was the unique means to transcend the absurdity of time passing and to win a kind of immortality. Their faith in the unique poetic vision that each individual might articulate was an article of faith in a life after death, a defiance of mortality. And it is not without good reason that in the weeks before his death McGahern said he was rereading Chateaubriand's *Mémoires*.

The paraphrase of Proust's essay highlights what McGahern felt was most interesting in it for him:

> What it says about Chateaubriand is that...when he is being clever and being man of the world, when he is being witty and entertaining, he is a good journalist; but when Chateaubriand says that this blue flower on the heath will have a second Spring, but I will have no second Spring, that is actually what one reads Chateaubriand for. While he is saying that he will have no second life, that is the one moment when he does have an immortal life. Then we actually hear the voice that is Chateaubriand's and no other voice.[34]

The distinction between good journalism and 'what one reads Chateaubriand for' is crucial and definitive. It is not simply that the decades Chateaubriand spent as a public man in French political life are of little importance; his charming recollection of it is equally so, for it is clear that in neither arena did he achieve 'an immortal life'. His immortality is in what Proust calls his poetry and in defining what a poet is:

> He tells us that nothing is on earth, soon he will die, oblivion will bear him off; we feel that what he says is true, for he is a man among men; but suddenly among these events, these ideas, through the mystery of his nature, he has discovered the poetry which was his unique object, and now the thought that was to have saddened us and we feel not that he will die but that he lives, that he is something superior to things, to events, to the years, and we smile when we reflect that this something is the same thing that we had loved in him already. This very permanence intoxicates us, for we feel that there is something higher than events, nothingness, death, the futility of everything.[35]

Proust goes on to say that Chateaubriand discovered this poetic essence in himself 'by dint of sincerity' and reaffirms his stirring faith in poetic vision: 'It is impossible to say why this reality is superior to that of a quite different order which gives to events their historical importance, to ideas their intellectual value even, even the realities of death and nothingness. Yet there is in it something that is more than those events.'[36] Already it is clear that Proust writes as a reader who has felt this superior reality, and that he will not define it in abstraction; in *Contre Sainte-Beuve* and in *À la recherche du temps perdu*, he will tap the poetic essence that he has in himself, and that work will be his proof that he can be superior to death and nothingness.

It is easy to see why the young McGahern would be attracted to such ideas so that they would become articles of faith for the rest of his life; easy to see also how much *The Barracks* owes to such a way of thinking, for in the character of the dying Elizabeth Reegan he embodies the figure of the poet achieving his own immortality. For a time, the voracious reader immersed himself in a wide body of European literature—Mann, Stendhal, Rilke, all the classic names appear—and may have refined his conviction wherever he found further evidence to reinforce it. Eventually he would recognize Proust's writings as his bible, and yet, as Proust insisted, it was not the intellectual articulation of an idea that mattered, nor being a good journalist, but the use of images that arose in one's deepest memory to make something beautiful. With this warning in mind, Proust became McGahern's mentor:

> So long as reading is treated as a guide holding the keys that open doors to buried regions of ourselves into which, otherwise, we should never penetrate, the part it can play in our lives is salutary. On the contrary, it becomes dangerous when, instead of waking us to the reality of our own mental processes, it becomes a substitute for them: when truth appears to us, not as an ideal which we can realize only as a result of our own thinking and our own emotional efforts, but as a material object which exists between the pages of a book.[37]

When McGahern came to write his 'Prologue' to his work in the mid-1960s, almost every sentence in it echoed Proust, but even more important is how often Proust returned to his mind as he wrote the fiction, and right up to his final work.[38]

It may be that McGahern's interest in Proust was what brought his attention back to Samuel Beckett, for there was an overt link between the two writers: Beckett's early essay on Proust, published in Paris in 1931. Just as McGahern immersed himself in Proust, reading not only the novel but also letters and essays as they appeared in translation, it is likely that he also read widely in Beckett's work. It was only with the publication in English of Beckett's prose, however, that McGahern would be able to gain a clear sense of Beckett's art and vision. The worldwide success of *Waiting for Godot* led to the publication of the post-war fiction, at first by the Olympia Press in Paris. *Molloy* came out in late 1955 and was banned in Ireland. *Malone Dies* was published in London in 1956 and *The Unnamable* in 1959. Shorter prose pieces also began to appear in little magazines, including 'L'Image' in 1959, in the first issue of the new magazine *X: A Quarterly Review of Literature and the Arts*, edited by Patrick Swift and David Wright. The plays were also appearing from Faber and Faber, *Waiting for Godot* in 1956, *All That Fall* in 1957, and *Endgame* in 1958. The brief book on Proust, which had been published in Paris in 1931, now also reappeared, and, as McGahern remarked, 'it tells more about Beckett than it tells about Proust'.[39]

Many of Beckett's concerns in his study of Proust reappear in *Godot* and other post-war work. While much of his discussion elucidates elements of Proust's novel, the style does not lend itself to extended or even serious analysis—he begins with references to 'the garrulous old dowager of the Letters' and to the 'abominable edition of the *Nouvelle Revue Française*'. Instead, Beckett's investigation of the ideas embedded in Proust's art is a virtuoso performance in a voice keyed to paradox and irony, irreverence, and mockery; it is as if he takes to heart Proust's own warning about reading, that it be an 'initiation', an 'incitement', to the recognition of one's own spiritual life. Inserted at many points are epigrammatic declarations that identify key convictions of Beckett, and these are some of the ideas that link him to both Proust and McGahern: 'We are alone. We cannot know and we cannot be known'; 'What is common to present and past is more essential than either taken separately. Reality, whether approached imaginatively or empirically, remains a surface, hermetic...the Proustian solution consists...in the negation of Time and Death, the negation of Death because the negation of Time'; 'Proust does not deal in concepts, he pursues the Idea, the concrete...the object may be a living symbol, but a symbol of itself'; 'Proust is positive only in so far as he affirms the value of intuition'; 'For Proust, as for the painter, style is more a question of vision than of technique...the quality of language is more important than any system of ethics or aesthetics'.[40]

Many of these ideas will be echoed in McGahern's later critical writing and are also embedded in *The Barracks*, *The Dark* and *Nightlines*, where the Beckettian influence is most discernible.[41] The mask of intellectual supremacy which the youthful Beckett adopted is partly a reflection of his masters, Proust and Joyce, but the post-war work is marked by a subversion of such a note; indeed, it is characterized by a noticeable humility. *Godot* and the prose work are focused on various forms of impotence: the yearning for intellectual clarity and order and the failure to achieve it; the desire to find a narrative shape for a life and the cyclical abandonment of such an endeavour; the need for intimacy and a measure of mutual understanding through language and the ultimate loneliness and incomprehension of separate selves; the incessant play of consciousness and the futility of making plans. It is arguable that while McGahern may have valued the philosophical positions articulated by Proust and Beckett, he would not have been drawn to either of them if they had not been most fundamentally aware of human frailty, vulnerability, and the mystery of human mortality.

If death is the defining condition of life, then the greatest challenge is to find an appropriate way of living with it—the goal that McGahern set himself in *The Barracks* and the other fiction of the 1960s. In this sense, any of Beckett's 'solitaries' trying to put a shape on their lives, imprisoned in their own thoughts, may have been in McGahern's mind as he imagined the life of Elizabeth Reegan. Her reflections, like those of Malone, are a kind of testament, a 'reckoning' of what her life has been and is. While Malone wishes to escape from 'the wild beast of earnestness' to the intellectual and imaginative 'play' with which he passes the time, Elizabeth is not quite so self-conscious about her reflections. Malone constantly returns to 'myself abandoned, in the dark without anything to play with', but Elizabeth is still in the busy world of the barracks home, of Reegan, the policemen and their wives, and of the children. They are going about their own lives, governed by routines and habits, clichés and

frustrations. Elizabeth finds herself reflecting on the contrast between herself and Reegan, and these words of Malone may point to
the central drama of their separate lives: 'Somewhere in this turmoil
thought struggles on, it too wide of the mark. It too seeks me, as it
always has, where I am not to be found. It too cannot be quiet. On
others let it wreak its dying rage, and leave me in peace.'[42] Reegan's
furiously driven campaign against his superior, Quirke, is a constant
irritant to the dying Elizabeth, who craves only a calm outlook on
her inevitable end.

On the first page of *Nightlines*, following a brief, overheard anecdote about a failed suicide attempt (surely a deliberate echo of an
episode in *Godot*), the protagonist of 'Wheels' remarks: 'Looked at
with the mind, life's a joke; and felt, it's a tragedy and we know
cursed nothing.'[43] While in sardonic Beckettian terms, the challenge
that is announced here is how to play the 'endgame', and McGahern
was certainly able to strike that note in some of the stories in *Nightlines*, and at times in *The Barracks* also, yet, in appreciating Beckett's
cleansing and fortifying vision of life and death—his 'elemental
spareness'[44]—the remark that 'you never meet place names in Beckett's books' points to a crucial distinction which McGahern preserved: the concrete reference embodied in a place name was for
him a sign of the recoverable hospitality of the world. But this distinction is most palpable in Elizabeth Reegan's bleak journey in *The
Barracks*, and McGahern's dialogue with Beckett is also palpable in
that novel. In the end, he would not imitate Beckett in his work, any
more than he would imitate Proust or Yeats but, in their dedication
to a spiritual search and a clear aesthetic project, all of them were
inspiring presences, and his own artistic commitments were honed
in a dialogue with them.

6

The Character of the Local Artist

There is no doubt that McGahern's response to much of Patrick
Kavanagh's work was admiration, coloured by what he detected as
the spiritual and personal cost of overcoming his impoverished circumstances in County Monaghan to make 'one of the longest journeys ever taken in Ireland, and in a bad time'. In his references to
Kavanagh's poetry, he is usually celebratory, but he also makes
clear that his observation of Kavanagh in his Dublin circles led him
to be less than admiring of the man and the cultural phenomenon
of which he was the focus and inspiration.

In learning to be a writer himself, to protect and refine his talent,
to accomplish the self-conquest of the artist, his observation of
Kavanagh in the late 1950s and early 1960s taught McGahern
much about the literary life. Part of the excitement of Kavanagh's
presence, he writes, was due to his 'violent energy', and the words
betray McGahern's fascination with his character as a father to
younger writers, but McGahern's experience of his own father's
'violent energy' had made him wary:

> With his extraordinary physical presence and overflowing
> energy, watching Kavanagh sitting alone in a chair was more
> like watching a warring crowd than a single solitary presence.
> Many of these presences can be found in the *Collected Poems*:
> the messiah ('there are people in the street who steer by my
> star'), the scourge of mediocrity and dullness, the humorist,
> the jaunty public man, the satirist.[1]

McGahern borrows John Arden's words about Kavanagh to convey
what he observed in McDaid's and other pubs: 'a fierce, aging face,
dark with anger, suddenly towering up under a shapeless hat from
among a group of men crowded round a table'.[2] The authority of

this presence is what fascinates McGahern, for, clearly, he kept his distance, even when others he respected surrendered to Kavanagh's forthright character.

McGahern reports that when Patrick Swift encouraged him to see more of this 'man of some genius', he replied that 'I had no inclination to go through the barrage of insult and abuse that seemed the necessary initiation to the doubtful joy of Kavanagh's company and that I preferred to read the work.' Swift had undergone that initiation and survived, but McGahern refused, as a scene in the story 'Bank Holiday' makes plain. McGahern concludes on the difficult character of Kavanagh: 'I think [Swift] understood perfectly the mixture of child and monster, fool and knave that went into the wayward intelligence of Kavanagh's genius. Out of the understanding has grown a deep, comic sympathy.'[3] McGahern shared his view of the character, but he had no wish to place himself voluntarily in a subservient position to an egocentric bully. The harshness of his rejection of Kavanagh—'he could go and inflate his great mouse of an ego somewhere else'—is perhaps a measure of how deeply his own father's power still disturbed him.[4]

There was a liveliness in Kavanagh's outspoken opinions, however, which evoked 'the possibility that literature could belong again to the streets rather than to the Church and University and the worn Establishment'. So much McGahern could admire, but he is acute in his analysis of how Kavanagh fell victim to this role of prophet, a man with a message, in whom liveliness often yielded to a 'not unusual Irish strategy': 'his message always had to define itself more by what it was against—dullness, insincerity, solemnity—than by what it was'.[5] In fact, McGahern thinks that this was no more than a stance, 'a general flailing about', because 'what this message was he never managed to make clear'. There were some who believed there was a message, whereas McGahern thinks it simply supported Kavanagh's work by preserving the 'passionate heart': 'it provided a platform that lifted the important poems; in the weaker poems it often appears as posturing'.

It is clear that McGahern believes that Kavanagh's followers encouraged him in this 'posturing' and that his best work is independent of any set message. Kavanagh's biographer Antoinette Quinn documents his sad descent into alcoholism and boorish behaviour, and the erosion of his talent, but McGahern is sympathetic to the incoherence of his life attributable to his social origins. He sees Kavanagh as rather like D. H. Lawrence, both of whom 'emerged roughly, from the same background into a society in which they felt, or were made to feel, outsiders. There are other similarities: their passionate care for genuineness of feeling, their violent reaction to bourgeois art and society, their hatred of the smug response.' He sees him finally in the words of Auden on Lawrence, as an 'anarchist rebel, who refuses to accept conventional laws and pieties as binding or worthy of respect'. These judgements were written by McGahern in the mid-1980s, looking back thirty years at the poet who meant so much to him but who was, in the end, stunted in his development, remaining, like Lawrence, a kind of infant, 'naïve and personal, as yet uncorrupted by education and convention'.[6]

These later discriminations of McGahern clarify much of his own efforts in the late 1950s to find his place. His orientation was to try to combine the 'genuineness of feeling' with 'conventional laws and pieties'; he was not an anarchist with a message or a bohemian. He honoured the 'individual vision' but was sure that it could be kept constant only by a rigorous self-discipline. There was little of the Romantic prophet about him, and though by background he resembles in ways Lawrence and Kavanagh, he seemed to value literary traditions and education much more than they did. This was not the education available in either St Patrick's Training College or University College Dublin, but the kind of literary education he had set out to create for himself, according to the highest classical standards. 'A single visit to McDaid's was enough to cure me of any desire for literary company for a month.' His caustic comment in *Memoir* makes clear that his education would not be found in these pubs, or from those who frequented them, and that his path would be a solitary one, supported, he says, by 'good friends within the city, individuals like myself'.[7] He read Kavanagh with care and thought deeply about his significance in the literary life of the city, but he makes clear that in his own journey out of his country background he would find his own way.

It was well known among young graduates of training colleges that they could gain an increase in salary by completing a bachelor's degree at university, and so, in 1956, as soon as McGahern knew that he was going to be living in Clontarf, he enrolled for an evening degree at University College Dublin. He may have hoped that the university would offer him the intellectual formation that had been missing in St Pat's, and the palpable excitement of early 1956, when he realized that there was a vibrant intellectual culture in the city, may have led him to want to enter into a larger community of intellectually gifted people like himself.

Teachers were exempted from the first year of the three-year degree programme if they passed an examination in Latin. McGahern passed this examination in the summer of 1956 and in the autumn began to attend lectures in English, Irish, and Economics. He continued with these subjects until his graduation in 1958. *Memoir* records nothing of his time at UCD, what he read, who his lecturers were, or whom he met, and, while this silence may be appropriate for the kind of memoir he wrote, it is not a reason to conclude that nothing of importance happened at the college. Elsewhere, he put on record his low opinion of the lectures he attended and, somewhat pointedly, named George O'Brien, Professor of Economics, as his most impressive teacher. O'Brien was an eloquent public speaker and took an interest in debate through, for instance, participation in the L&H, the Literary and Historical Society, the celebrated university forum, which McGahern certainly attended.

In English, the programme of study in these years followed the Oxford model, so that the prescribed texts for study were the traditional canon: Chaucer's 'Prologue to the *Canterbury Tales*', many plays by Shakespeare, extracts from *Paradise Lost*, Palgrave's *Golden Treasury of Songs and Lyrics*, Clarendon Press selections of Bacon, Dryden, Swift, Samuel Johnson, Wordsworth, Shelley, Keats, Burke's *Reflections on the Revolution in France*, and Cardinal Newman's *University Sketches*. Over the two years, lectures on all these texts were given, but how many of them McGahern attended, or how carefully he read these classic works is not known. He might have made a judicious selection of the works for intensive study in the weeks before the final examinations, but the list itself reinforces the coherence of the literary tradition to which he was exposed as a young man in all educational institutions. The notions of tradition and the classic literary work were constantly reinforced, and references crop up later in his life to many of these writers. While there is no doubt that McGahern was widely read, and these texts are a background, known and absorbed, the works he discovered for himself certainly had the deeper impact. His reading may not have been precisely segregated in this way, however, and it is worth noting that one of the required texts in his Irish course was *An tOileánach*. Although he was familiar with it from St Pat's as a modern classic in Irish, it is unlikely that he would associate it at this time with Beckett's oeuvre, although he had made this connection by the late 1960s, long before he wrote in praise of the Blasket Islands memoir.

It appears that the teaching in the English and Irish Departments left little that was memorable or that felt life-defining, although it is significant that there were no novels or short stories on the reading list, and so fiction remained in the domain of private reading. The self-education in his 'freemasonry', already underway by this time, was an impassioned solitary endeavour, and so it is not surprising that routine class-work would seem scarcely worth his time. It is likely that the young teacher continued to follow the BA programme purely as a means of gaining a qualification to augment his small salary. Yet, apart from some fellow-students, there were lecturers in the Department of English who were as enthusiastic about litera- ture, writing, and drama as he was. In their own ways, they contrib- uted to the ambience of the university and were committed to current writing and to the literary vocation itself. Among them were Denis Donoghue, Roger McHugh, John Jordan, and Lorna Reynolds. In some cases, it seems that McGahern impressed them with his work or in other ways became friendly with some of the younger faculty members, who were presided over by Professor J. J. Hogan, a figure in the literary establishment, and a member of awards com- mittees of the Arts Council and of the controversial Censorship Appeal Board.

More important than the others in practical ways was Roger McHugh, who, in addition to lecturing, was a dramatist and drama critic. He was a nationalist, whose plays were usually embedded in the Republican narrative, but he was a controversial figure in the university and outside. He had crossed swords publicly with Michael Tierney, the ultra-Catholic Chancellor of the university, and with Ernest Blythe, the manager of the Abbey Theatre, when he had picketed the theatre to draw attention to its declining standards.

McHugh's importance for McGahern was his independence and courage, and he recognized and promoted McGahern's fiction at the beginning by publishing an extract from work in progress in 1961–2. McHugh's enthusiastic support may have indirectly played a part in the awarding of the prizes McGahern received in 1962 and 1964, and they remained in contact through the controversy in 1965 concerning the banning of *The Dark* and McGahern's dismissal from his teaching position.

In spite of his general disaffection and declared independence from the university, the young teacher's confidence may have grown through his presence there. Some members of the Kavanagh circle and, later, of the milieu of Mary Lavin overlapped with the university, and so he was enabled to get an insider's sense of how these circles touched and how he belonged or, indeed, did not.

In the spring of 1958, when Michael McLaverty attended the English Literature Society at UCD, McGahern went to see the Northern novelist 'since I'd read and enjoyed all of his books'.[8] Like Kavanagh, McLaverty was born on a small farm in County Monaghan early in the century. He was of the generation of McGahern's mother and his fiction had been published for twenty years in London and New York with moderate critical success; he had trained as a teacher in Belfast and during these decades had balanced the roles of writer and teacher. 'He spoke confidently and forcefully, with dry humour, patent sincerity and, above all, kindliness', McGahern recalled much later, these words suggesting that in McLaverty he may have seen a figure who was the opposite of Kavanagh. In recalling the discussion on that occasion, which appears to have followed conventional topics, 'O'Connor and O'Faolain and the Russians...the neglect of Daniel Corkery, especially the stories', McGahern reveals that it was the personality of the man that attracted him. In a 'bluff headmasterly manner', McLaverty threw out a challenge to the students—to read Corkery's stories and to write to him if they agreed with his own high estimate of them. 'I had liked *The Threshold of Quiet*', McGahern recalled, 'but had been put off by the nationalistic essays, which at the time were more in vogue than the fiction.' Yet it is clear that he wanted to get in touch with McLaverty, took up his challenge, and discovered that he liked one story in particular, 'Vision'. Eventually, in January 1959, he sent the opening letter in what would become an important correspondence and friendship.

That McGahern should initiate a correspondence is in itself striking and there are clues that he did so out of a need to distance himself from the Dublin writers he already knew. 'The originality of Kavanagh's talent [McLaverty] noticed from the beginning, but felt that after *The Great Hunger* and *A Soul for Sale*, Kavanagh had gone wrong in Dublin. "Poor Kavanagh", he would murmur. He had a Northerner's view of Dublin as an envious, idle, incestuous, destructive place, and approved of Cyril Connolly's description: "A warm pool full of smiling crocodiles".'[9] An early letter makes clear that Kavanagh was a reference point and that both were frank in their assessment; McGahern writes: 'I was sorry to see Patrick Kavanagh make a fool of himself about your writing; though I don't expect you minded your name being linked with Hardy's. Kavanagh is an irresponsible critic and a careless poet. It's a pity he doesn't take more care with his poems because he is richly gifted.'[10] The critical confidence of this assessment reveals how much McGahern had already placed himself outside the Kavanagh coterie and how much he trusted McLaverty to understand. '[McLaverty] was as far from Bohemia as he was from the salon', McGahern observed in a formulation that seems to chart his own course somewhere between Kavanagh and Proust.

The engaged energy of these letters written by the unpublished McGahern, and then, in the heat of first success in the early 1960s, belies the more detached tone of respect in the recollections decades later. Beginning some years earlier in St Pat's, he tells McLaverty, he discovered his novels and many of the stories and reaffirmed his admiration for them in paying tribute to the novelist later, 'a poet who worked in prose and honoured that medium'. In the opening letter, McGahern tells him that *Truth in the Night* gave him most enjoyment but that *School for Hope* 'is the novel I think greatest'. 'For many chapters, I thought *The Choice* was to be your best novel.' It is evident in such remarks that McGahern has studied the novels and stories with care and is capable of sharp critical distinctions, all, however, in tribute to a writer whose 'books have given me a better appreciation of life as well as their own pleasure'. It is clear that he feels an integrity of vision and a care for art that is rooted in its dramatization: 'I believe that it is a great achievement for any man to state, even once, a measure of his experience truthfully.'[11]

The first novel of McLaverty that he read had a major impact on him: 'I read it several times that month', he told the author. It may be worthwhile to wonder why *Truth in the Night* would appeal so much to the young student recently moved away from the country that he would make a study of McLaverty's whole work in the following years. It is a narrative of an enclosed island community whose traditional way of life is ending as the younger generation emigrates. The central characters confound this migration: Martin, who returns after fifteen years away, and Vera, a woman of the mainland who married an islander and is now widowed. To stay, to return, or to leave are the decisions that animate the drama. A small cast of characters, some bitterly at odds, and deeply dissatisfied with their lot, others with a cast of mind that allows them to be generous and loving, are all revealed in their inner selves by a wise clarity of psychological awareness. The novel is Hardyesque in its sense of the tragic fates that overwhelm everybody; individuals are at the mercy of nature and illness, and, although there is a Catholic ethic that suggests that it is the will of God that must be divined and accepted, this is not a doctrinal novel. While it is actually set on an island off the coast of Antrim, it might be Synge's Aran Islands, or the Blaskets, or, indeed, any bleak sea coast, for there is an elemental quality about the forces that surround and shape the characters and their limited lives. The poetic vision of McLaverty is embodied in a narrative and setting, which, in retrospect, can be seen to mirror McGahern's own abiding concerns. 'To read it was like coming into a new country', McGahern wrote, as if he realized that he had left behind the Ireland he had known and a new Ireland in art was unveiled before him, a local world in which a moral drama of classic grandeur took place.

In March 1960, after McLaverty and he had met for the first time, in Dublin, McGahern wrote that 'one of the things that overjoyed me was not to feel that there was much difference between the man and his work'.[12] It is certainly a recurring aspect of all good writing that McGahern seeks: an absolute grounding of style in sincere feeling—although, of course, the nature of the technique which dramatizes that feeling is the crucial issue if one is to avoid

the sentimentality of self-expression or the performative accomplishment of the professional writer. On this occasion, McLaverty rec-
ommended Seán O'Faolain's *Bird Alone*, but McGahern's dismissal
of it is forthright, in spite of its skill: 'I couldn't like it...It has always
seemed phoney to me—the man in the work. Somewhere in his
journals Da Vinci says "an unskilful man who is honest is far more
likely to achieve something than a great craftsman who has no honesty".'[13] It is clear that, unlike O'Faolain, McLaverty embodied such
honesty, a primary quality of the artist whose 'moments of vividness,
of beauty and truth', are 'scattered throughout all the books', and
the writers who were his absolute touchstones were Tolstoy and
Chekhov. The journal entries that trace McLaverty's thinking surely
mirror his declarations to McGahern: 'In literature nothing fades so
quickly as falsity and nothing wears so well as truth...By thinking
deeply, by feeling, one gathers that out of suffering and sacrifice and
unselfishness come happiness: the defeat of egoism, the futility of
violence, the effect of kindness.'[14] In such conclusions about the
necessary devotion to the deepening of the artist's character many
of McGahern's future beliefs are anticipated.

Seamus Heaney worked as a young teacher in McLaverty's school
in Belfast for a year, 1961–2, and Heaney's brief celebration of the
man and his work later puts the relationship in an interesting light.
He recalled McLaverty's enthusiasm for literature: 'he writes and talks
with an artist's passion'.[15] Heaney remembered that the older man
exhorted him to read Tolstoy's 'The Death of Ivan Ilyich'—'one of
his sacred texts'—as he had exhorted McGahern a few years earlier:
'if fidelity to the intimate and the local is one of [McLaverty's] obvious strengths as a writer, another is his sense of the great tradition that
he works in, his contempt for the flashy and the topical, his love of
the universal, the worn grain of unspectacular experience, the well-
turned grain of language itself'. Heaney situated McLaverty in ways
that surely echo McGahern and confirm his shrewd sense of 'the
mastery in his voice' behind 'the modesty of its pitch'. Even more,
Heaney may be putting his finger on the aspect that meant most to
McGahern: 'a comprehension of the central place of suffering and
sacrifice in the life of the spirit'. Such words suggest how knowing
McLaverty and his work so well at the time he wrote *The Barracks*
contributed to the clarity and power of his vision in that novel.

But McLaverty's 'honesty' was limited. 'Apart from his talent and intelligence', McGahern wrote after McLaverty's death in 1992:

I believe that he was perfectly in tune with the simplicities of the Catholicism and green Nationalism he had grown up in, and those beliefs he adhered to piously throughout his long life. As well as being a source of strength, they may have taken some toll. In the novels, in particular, there is sometimes a turning away from any disturbing grain in the material into the safe/unsafe paths of convention.[16]

As McGahern moved from *The Barracks* to *The Dark*, he entered a territory of which McLaverty could not approve, and McGahern experienced a 'turning away' in McLaverty's response to the latter novel. The early letters show genuine warmth, however, between these men of different generations, a trust and a pleasure in knowing each other. 'I wrote because I owe much to your own work, of living Irish prose writers I admire your works most', McGahern began, and even though he realized by the mid-1960s that his work was growing beyond the scope of McLavery's literary sensibility, he retained considerable esteem for his art and for his character.

Heaney's remark on McLaverty's 'fidelity to the intimate and the local' and his simultaneous 'love of the universal' identifies a central strand of McGahern's own developing identity. Kavanagh's insistence on the 'provincial' as a critical category, as opposed to the 'national', was well known, and while McGahern devoted much time to French traditions of writing in search of a technique that would capture the 'universal', he also developed his own tradition of the local or 'provincial'. Kavanagh and McLaverty were part of that tradition from the beginning, but over the years, and especially after the 1970s McGahern's marked interest in local writing emerges again, most notably, perhaps, in his praise of Ó Criomhthain's *An tOileánach / The Islandman* and many other 'island' writers, but also in his affection for a writer like Jane Austen. In the early years, the distinctive local worlds of Kavanagh and McLaverty were recognizably close to home, especially in their piety and Catholicism, or more generally in the cultural expression of that faith. They wrote of the moral and spiritual world of McGahern's parents and grandparents, and two other local writers of an earlier generation also appealed to him at this time, both of them with a decidedly 'period' and local identity.

McGahern's first contact with McLaverty came about because of the Belfast writer's championing of Daniel Corkery's short stories, and it is arguable that both writers capture something of the spiritual ethos of his own mother. One of the few books she had in her house when McGahern was a child was Corkery's novel *The Threshold of Quiet*. In view of McGahern's later praise of the novel, and of stories by Corkery, it is interesting to think of it as a significant period novel. The epigraph is taken from Thoreau: 'The mass of men lead lives of quiet desperation', and the title alludes to this sentence. Corkery's depiction of a set of overlapping lives in turn-of-the-century Cork is a narrative in which incompletion, despair, emigration, and death are the lot of these largely passive and withdrawn characters. The central character, Martin, is ineffectually in love with Lily. At her father's funeral, he observes her eyes: 'On the deck of a liner, in a hospital ward, in a railway carriage, such faces are to be seen; the faces of those who have to dare a future they had thought about, but not with certainty. Upon them an aspect of stillness seems to be ever deepening into far-away abstraction. There is one phrase to describe the look—quiet desperation.'[17]

The novel opens with a suicide; Martin draws spiritual sustenance from *The Imitation of Christ*, the classic handbook of Catholic meditation by Thomas à Kempis; Lily's brother considers joining the priesthood, and Lily herself decides to become a nun. Corkery appears to demonstrate that a form of Catholic contemplative response is inevitable in these circumstances, 'desperation' perhaps redeemed by 'quietness'. Most remarkable in tracing a certain affinity between this novel and McGahern's work is the concluding paragraph:

> It was a night of perfect stillness. Outside the water-birds fluttered over the lake... The room was filled with quietness; not with the quietness of peace, it may be, but then it is not the quietness of peace that leaves men's souls gentle and deep and rich, even if just a little, a very little, pensive, not to say bitter. Bitter! but when such souls quit our company it is the sweetness of their quiet spirits that remains like a fragrance in the air.[18]

The 'stillness' and 'perfect stillness' on the lake seem to anticipate the opening paragraph of *That They May Face the Rising Sun*, although the notion of a 'quiet spirit' might describe the character of Elizabeth Reegan in *The Barracks*.

Equally remarkable in Corkery's depiction of a Catholic contemplative ethos of spiritual exile is that he drew his epigraph from the American Protestant transcendentalist Thoreau, and that the final phrase, which describes that 'quietness', is 'a fragrance in the air'. This is a clear echo of Forrest Reid, a Protestant novelist from Belfast with a transcendental orientation. One of McGahern's favourite phrases for the spiritual life was 'moral fragrance', taken from Reid's book on Yeats. What all these writers have in common is a contemplative spiritual outlook of the *fin de siècle*, commonly associated with this 'threshold of quiet', and in its Protestant version often associated with spiritualism and the supreme reality of the afterlife of the soul. It may not be too much to suggest that McGahern consciously associated the style of this literary ethos with his mother, and above all with Yeats's poetry of the 1890s, of the 'Celtic Twilight' period.

McGahern's attraction to regional writers is more marked in his consistent attraction to Forrest Reid's characteristic style over a twenty-year period. Reid became a touchstone in a way that the author of *The Threshold of Quiet* never did; Corkery's later sectarian and exclusionary views on Irish writing were distasteful to McGahern. The Belfast writer had a considerable reputation earlier in the century—and his work was known to McLaverty—but his books were going out of print in the 1950s. McGahern reports that he found Reid's memoir *Apostate* on the book-barrow on Henry Street, and then read a second volume of memoirs, *Private Road*, before interesting himself in Reid's career. Certain parallels between Reid's early life and that of McGahern become evident in *Apostate*, which may account for McGahern's early interest in him, but he will become fascinated by certain qualities of Reid's style. In the mid-1960s and again in the mid-1970s, he will try to interest publishers in reprinting a novel, *Brian Westby*, and then will write an essay about it for Reid's centenary, all this to show that the affection he had for Reid was lasting, and so one must assume that he struck a chord when McGahern first discovered him.

It is a measure of the intellectual independence of the young McGahern that he would take precious time off from reading Proust and Flaubert to read with care a minor figure found by chance. The essay—one of the very few he wrote—includes some indirect explanations, but it was written in 1975 and certainly reflects some of his current preoccupations. *Brian Westby*, he wrote, reminded him of Thomas Mann's *Death in Venice* and Herman Hesse's *Demian*:

> [These novels by Mann and Hesse] are both romantic and written within an established tradition. This Forrest Reid did not have…Yet, Forrest Reid has what is more in this ideal, never far and never lost in the beautiful rhythmical prose, a true and permanent voice. And for all its flaws as a work, this voice rings out more powerfully and poignantly in parts of *Brian Westby* than perhaps anywhere else in Reid's works.[19]

He goes on to invoke an image from a letter of Proust, a commonplace in McGahern's later commentaries, the church spire 'which lifts men's eyes from the avaricious earth': 'Such a spire is still at the heart of *Brian Westby* and all Reid's work. That spire is but a symbol of what Reid himself has beautifully called a moral fragrance.'[20] This is the highest praise McGahern could offer, to discover this vital spiritual quality in a work, and 'moral fragrance' joined Proust's spire in his evaluative vocabulary.

While his appreciation of this quality of voice in Reid's work is central to the essay, McGahern spends much time quoting a long passage from the novel which, he says, is a 'perfect description of suffering', and other passages which remind him of Henry James or Hardy. The central character is a novelist, and at one point Westby expresses his credo as an artist in words that echo McGahern:

> There must be something behind—or rather all *through* your work—a spiritual atmosphere. It seems to me that this alone can give it richness. Art isn't just life in the raw: it is a selection from life: it is a vision:—life seen through a temperament, as Zola said. And its quality depends on the quality of the temperament far more than the material out of which the actual pattern is woven.[21]

This McGahern may endorse fully, but he is strict in his judgement of how the novel is constructed, its mechanical and improbable plotting, dishonest characterization, and more.

Wishing to understand what is wrong with the novel, and all Reid's work, McGahern formulates a theory that is surely autobiographical in its resonance. It is a theory about literary tradition:

> Rich as his best work is in its echoes of great pastoral poetry, as well as the prose rhythms of Henry James and Jane Austen in the delicate sense of timing, the voice might never have become individual without the tension of being Irish, of being outside the tradition he knew and loved; and he might have become just another English writer of no very great distinction. Or, freed of the tension by being born within the tradition, his work might have been more fully realized, less warped.[22]

These are the thoughts of the novelist who had recently finished *The Leavetaking*, and there are traces of these thoughts in that novel, but it is possible to go back to those first years, when he was reading Proust and Yeats intensively, and see why he might take time over Reid. Thoughts on the ambivalent relationship of an Irish-born writer to an English tradition of fiction must surely belong in McGahern's search for his own place in the many literary traditions he was uncovering. Reid's admiration of Yeats's work would have interested McGahern at that time, and he may have already begun to reflect on what he would later refer to as a Northern Irish spirituality, which he found also in the work of Louis MacNeice and McLaverty. Already one can see McGahern seeking out local writing and cultural contexts for his own sensibility, and even though his immersion in French and modernist literature had a major influence on his work, in later decades he will focus increasingly on finding how a style for a 'universal' literature may be won from 'local' material.

Memoir records that McGahern 'drifted from the Church. So imperceptibly did it happen that it was not clear even to me whether I had left the Church or the Church had left me.'[23] The literary echo in this remark and other literary echoes in the passage that follows in explanation suggest that the separation was effortless and that his complex relationship to the 'sacred weather' of his upbringing was, in the end, simple and obvious. He had a 'lack of any strong feeling' about 'superficial observances' and so he could attend mass or not attend as he judged the politics of a particular situation, but more generally, he insisted that he still had 'gratitude for my upbringing in the church'. It is a position he maintained throughout his life; while he was angry with the institutional Church and the theocracy it maintained in the country, its baleful anti-intellectual influence through such institutions as St Pat's and the schools system, or in its policing of sexual and reproductive matters through doctors and hospitals, for instance, he did not wish to challenge the spiritual tradition of the Church or the beliefs of the faithful.

In the matter of his own belief and the spiritual influence of the Church, he appears to have developed a complex attitude, and this attitude may have taken some time to evolve. On the one hand, he 'realized I was no longer dreaming' and he became a sceptical rationalist; over time, he will invoke some key figures in that tradition. He appears to have drawn particular support from David Hume's views on natural religion, and often invoked Hume's view that he does not discuss religion because it is a matter of belief; it is not a rational matter. More pointedly rational was Freud in viewing religion as an imaginative and perhaps necessary illusion. At the end of his life, McGahern will say that he agrees with Freud's argument in *The Future of an Illusion* about the narcissism of many illusions people choose to believe in, but in referring to Jung, it is clear that he is also sympathetic to the spiritual dimension in life: 'I think that without religion, life is, to a certain extent, impoverished.'[24]

In the 1950s, McGahern was emerging into his own independent intellectual life, and yet the Catholic ethos in which this was happening preserved in certain rebellious quarters a Catholic intellectual tradition. It is not altogether surprising that McGahern, whose second name at baptism was Augustine, would read with appreciation the *Confessions* of St Augustine early in his life and respond favourably: 'Before I read Proust I was obsessed with that great passage on memory in St. Augustine's *Confessions*, which I think is the best part of the *Confessions*. I think it's one of the greatest pieces of writing that ever was.'[25] Nor is it surprising that, like Joyce, he would be familiar with some of the ideas of St Thomas Aquinas. In particular, he—and Patrick Swift—refer with approval to Aquinas's statement on the image as the foundation of knowledge, and McGahern remarks, 'Out of memory is the image and, of course, memory is the basis of the imagination.'[26] In fact, in the number of *Nimbus* in 1956, which included the poems of Kavanagh, Patrick Swift had an essay, 'Some Notes on Caravaggio', in which he attempts to define the Catholic and Latin nature of the painter's imagination and to register his own passionate response to the paintings in these terms. Swift quoted from Proust and, in general, alludes to ideas about art, imagination, and religious vision which seem greatly imbued by a Catholic cultural formation.[27] While much attention was devoted in Irish literary criticism to the nationalist context, just as much was devoted to the Catholic and Latin connection, even by such liberal figures as Sean O'Faolain, Kate O'Brien, or Conor Cruise O'Brien, the author, writing as Donat O'Donnell, of a remarkable series of essays collected in *Maria Cross: Imaginative Patterns in a Group of Modern Catholic Writers.* While McGahern later ridiculed the idea that he and his friends would have any respect for naïve critical categories such as 'Irish Literature' or 'Catholic Literature', it remains true that the ethos in which he grew to maturity was permeated by such concerns, even at the most intellectually cultivated levels.[28]

His first statement of principles, 'The Image', briefly compares art and religion, and Freud's ideas may be reflected in his remarks on 'the illusory permanence of false gods'.[29] Art answers an 'instinctive need', just as religion does. He remarks that 'art betrays the simple religious nature of its activity' in its search for perfection and for the ideal, lost image. Religion rewards the believer with the promise of eternal life, whereas the reward of dedication to art is an individual style. It is clear that the closest human need and activity to the making of art is the practice of religion; by the late 1950s McGahern had made his choice, but in acknowledging the origin of belief in human need, he preserved a respect for these instincts that are so close to each other.

What is evident is that he came to view religious belief as a psychological and cultural phenomenon and that in reading philosophical or anthropological ideas he was drawn to the notion that irrational beliefs were necessary for most people because they were comforting in the face of the unknown forces that govern life; they 'make palatable the inexplicable'. He cited a book by E. R. Dodds,

The Greeks and the Irrational, as the source for a key distinction mentioned in *Memoir*: 'I had come to separate morals and religion, to see morals as simply our relationship with other people and the creatures of the earth and air, and religion as our relationship with our total environment, the all that surrounds our little life.'[30] Here he repeats a sentence he often quoted from Dodds's book, published in 1949 and almost certainly known in intellectual circles in Dublin. An Oxford scholar, Dodds was closely associated with the poet Louis MacNeice and the writer/philosopher Stephen McKenna. McGahern held him in high esteem. Dodds took an interest in spiritualism, another aspect of his life which McGahern commented on in referring to Dodds's autobiography.[31]

On the one hand, McGahern might be described as a sceptical rationalist with an anthropological interest in religion, but the lapsed Catholic preserved a very strong affinity with the sense of enveloping mystery. For Proust, Joyce, and Kavanagh, such a belief was inextricable from their imaginative power; their instinct for visionary language had a mystical and sacramental dimension. McGahern declared that he did not believe in an afterlife or in the immortality of the soul, yet from *The Barracks* to *That They May Face the Rising Sun* his fiction often associates a sense of the numinous with the landscape, with the earth itself as the site of human need and aspiration. While this might be an evocation of an aesthetic tradition, a form of Wordsworthian vitalism, in *Memoir* it takes on a more intimate, personal resonance. It is associated with memories of his mother in the landscape, and, again in *Memoir*, he distinguishes between the Catholic Church of darkness, associated with his father and an authoritarian and punitive tradition, and the Church of light, associated with his mother.

At the end of his life, the reason for his generous feelings towards the Catholic Church of his childhood, and his upbringing in it, is given: he associates it with his mother's faith, and the last words of that book declare: 'I would want no shadow to fall on her joy and deep trust in God.'[32] In the 1950s, then, when he challenged his father in many different ways in order to assert his own independence and freedom from the false authority of a patriarchal culture, a narcissistic culture as it appeared to him, he still preserved a reverence for the person and the beliefs of his mother. That reverence is rooted in a conviction that a 'true religious instinct' is an ineradicable part of human nature itself. In 1992 he declared: 'I don't believe, I don't go to church or partake in a formal religion. But I actually do think that it's a very important part of our civilization, part of my inheritance. I mean I don't think the Catholic Church is true any more than Buddhism is true, or, you know, any of the others, but they all express in different ways the same human need; and I see it as an important and essential need.'[33] Such reflections represent the attitude that first evolved in the 1950s and 1960s, and they anticipate his final novel, *That They May Face the Rising Sun.*

7

'The End or the Beginning of Love'

'Who do you love most of all, Jim?' The handwriting—large letter-ing, formal, open—suggests that this may be one of the first versions of all those fictions of a woman dying, registered here through the boy's consciousness. In this scene of the boy being questioned by the mother from her sickbed, the narrator is close to the child's feelings, and McGahern's interest in the scene is less in the dying mother, in the fact of her death, than in her impact on the boy. '"You, mother. No one near as much as you", he said, and by her smile it was what she had wanted and expected. She could do her duty freely now.' It is a ritual the boy knows well, the repetition itself a deadening of authentic feeling, but the boy's resentment of this distancing is the real focus; in fact, he appears betrayed by the mother's impersonal placing of duty before love. '"Remember, that's not right. There is One Person in the world that you must love before any other. Don't you remember, Jim?" "Yes", he admitted with some fear, the life sinking out of his face; it would be the Catechism Class all over again.' He 'parrots' the required answer, but the next question forces the issue to a more intimate crisis:

> 'I don't love our father as much as you', he burst out. 'It'd be lies to say anything else'.
>
> 'No. You must say what's right. To say what's right is never lies. Oh, Jim, you know I'm not well. Can't you say what's right for my sake?'
>
> 'I love my earthly father and mother equally', he admitted at last in a low resentful tone, his eyes fixed on the floor-boards. He spoke neither in his own voice or words...
>
> 'I knew you'd say what was right. There's a certain order laid down for us to follow: we can't pick our loves the way we

want them', she said, and she was prepared to be indulgent,
now that she had had her way.[1]

The conflict here between what the isolated individual feels and
'what's right'—or, perhaps, what is not circumscribed by the self—
will be a central drama in much of McGahern's fiction, at first here
between the person and the required role, and it is striking how
much the dying woman is almost a caricature of the parental role.
The boy is not only resentful of what he feels is her dishonesty and
her insistence that he too betray his personal feelings, but he becomes aware also of the power she wields over him and her satisfaction in using that power. Most striking of all here is the recognition
of the gap between what is felt and what is said. He is forced to
present himself publicly 'neither in his own voice or words'. The
need to have an authentic voice will be fulfilled in the writing of
fiction, not first, however, in the dramatization of the boy's inner life
but, most triumphantly, in the articulation in *The Barracks* of the
woman's true voice behind the dutiful words.

At various stages in the revision of the story, Jim became Stevie
and then Hugh, but while the boy is still Jim, there is a striking
foreshadowing of what will later become *The Barracks*. While the
narrative voice is close to the boy's consciousness, he is aware of
another consciousness: '"Don't worry, Jim", she said, and it seemed
for a while that she would try once more to share with him her own
knowledge of her going, as she had shared most of her life in the last
years with him, but she finally kissed him goodnight whispering not
to worry.' It is in this moment that one glimpses the crucial difference between *his* knowledge of her going, presented subjectively in
these fictions, and *her* knowledge of her going, something that
McGahern will have to imagine in *The Barracks*, but it is also clear
that he would never have been able to imagine 'her own knowledge'
if she had not shared with him already 'most of her life'.

In spite of his resentment of her power over him, he is in love
with her, and this contradiction will later become the heart of *The
Leavetaking*. In his note to the revised version of that novel, he comments on the difficulty of capturing in language the other consciousness, the beloved, the not 'I', and its 'purity of feeling'; he wonders
if 'these disparates could in any way be made true to one another'.

That preface, written in 1983, is evidence of how the central struggle throughout much of McGahern's career was the challenge of
moving beyond the autobiographical, the 'purity of feeling' of the
'I', to another kind of knowledge. He speaks of the challenge as a
matter of style, and this is also true in the broadest sense of style as
individual personality, the voice won in language out of the struggle
with oneself. That struggle began in 'The Going' and in trying to
find a way to write about his relationship with his mother.

How long this first stage will take, how many years of writing, or
what exactly the stages were in the revisions of this archetypal scene
are hard to pin down, for it is the long trajectory through the writing of 'The End or the Beginning of Love' to *The Barracks*, from, say,
1957 to 1961, that has to be imagined. There is a typed version
identical to the pages just quoted from, and then another episode,
describing the funeral, called 'The End', apparently a separate story,
although in other versions these two scenes are I and II of 'The
Going'. He appears to have worked on it again in late 1962, after
The Barracks was completed, when he sent the story to the *New Yorker*,
and it is likely that it was part of the earliest version of *The Leavetaking*
written some years before that novel was eventually completed in
1973–4. Thirty years later, this final section of Part I of *The Leavetaking* was incorporated with little revision into *Memoir*. McGahern's
lifelong preoccupation with this material is a clear indication that in
it he discovered the central spiritual issues of his work and also its
stylistic challenges.

The many versions of 'The Going' essentially dramatize the final
scenes of the parting of the boy from his mother and then her burial
in his absence. As in *The Leavetaking*, and thirty years later in *Memoir*,
the boy regrets that he leaves the room and wishes he had gone
back again to say goodbye once more, but what is remarkable here
in an early version is the transference of feeling to objects, a classic
McGahern poetic device in later years:

> It would break his heart to leave her again, he would not be
> able, his whole life would break into one mad cry of suffering,
> they'd have to drag him away. He watched the green scum of
> weed on the cinders, the blackcurrant bushes against the sag-
> ging wooden paling down from the turf shed, the young apple

trees circled with nettingwire to keep the goats from stripping the bark, and they came to him with such shocking vividness that they hurt, he'd never really seen things in their loss before.[2]

The lorry bears the children away from the house to the barracks, leaving the mother to die without her husband or children near her.

> People were saving hay in meadows along the road, or resting or eating in the shadows of the haycocks. Butterflies flickered white in the sunshine and the sweet scent of new hay lay over everything.
>
> Already his father's voice was in his ears, 'God, O God, O God, what will I do with the pack of you? What did I do to deserve this cross? God, O God, O God!' and he wished the lorry could go on and on and on so that he'd never have to stand on firm earth again.

The accomplishment of this writing is extraordinary already, years before McGahern finds the form in which to situate it. It is a writing out of personal memories, but already the keynote images of the countryside bear an extraordinary depth of feeling. The poetry of McGahern's style is already present, the 'shocking vividness' with which the frailty and overwhelming meaning of human life is rendered, although he has not yet found a way to situate these memories in relation to a unifying theme or form. 'The End or the Beginning of Love' marks a major step forward in writing this scene and in moving beyond it, both in the sense that the first chapter is a significant revision of 'The Going' and in the sense that the novel-length narrative is a study of the adolescent life of Hugh.

In the typescript sent to publishers in the summer of 1959, Hugh is the name given to the protagonist, formerly known as Jim and Stevie, and the narrative begins at the same point as 'The Going', the last weeks of the mother's life, but, in fact, only a few pages now remain of the thirty-eight pages in the story. The boy and his dying mother are envisaged quite differently, and the narrative continues after this opening chapter to follow Hugh's development in the ten years following his mother's death. The children move to live in the barracks with the father, who soon resigns from the police and buys a farm. Little attention is given to the life of the barracks, and as in *The Dark* and, later, in *Amongst Women*, the action of the novel is set on a farm. In this and other ways, the chronology of events does not correspond to their sequence in the history of the McGahern family as set out in *Memoir*.

The years pass: the father is frustrated and embittered, and is violent towards the boy and his sisters; Hugh has an important friendship with Campbell, he goes to secondary school in Carrick, his sisters grow up and move away to London—Maura being especially independent, sexually aware, and strong-willed—and their father quarrels with them by letter; Mahoney remarries, and his new wife is named Elizabeth. Hugh considers if he should become a priest and spends time at Father Gerald's house, as young Mahoney does in *The Dark*. He studies hard, fails to win a university scholarship, and so education is not depicted as an important part of his life, as it is in young Mahoney's life in *The Dark*; instead, the final four chapters follow the course of a troubled love affair with a young teacher, during which the issue of the priesthood and his religious belief are resolved. The novel ends with Hugh's departure from the farm to join his sisters in London.

A number of passages show considerable accomplishment in characterization and in the depiction of the family. The difference between 'The Going' and the opening chapter is striking and worth examining for it marks a movement forward in McGahern's way of treating the autobiographical experience and foreshadows the vision that will unify *The Barracks*. The most remarkable advance is that the narrator situates the boy's experience in a richly realized family context. While the relationship of boy and mother is important, the relationship of the mother and father is dramatized, the maid and Hugh's young siblings are all given attention, the bustle of people— the nurse, the aunt, the priest—around the sickroom is evoked, and the time is given very precisely, May–June; a thunder and lightning storm which frightens the boy is woven in; a Christmas scene—the last Christmas—is recalled with much detail of the games and toys with which the children occupied themselves. In short, the realism of the scene is carefully weighted, each person's consciousness is treated sympathetically and in an even-handed way, including the father, and while there are gut-wrenching moments as the mother's death approaches, the narrative perspective moves back to situate everyone's feelings in the larger picture of life continuing with its routines and rituals. It is tempting to think that this chapter is McGahern's most accomplished and most mature work to date, that it was worked on more and later than other parts of the novel, but this cannot be proven; what is evident is that the treatment of the death-house here has many signature features of much later fiction.

The treatment of the relationship of husband and wife has already marked stylistic and thematic features of *The Barracks*:

> The father came but seldom. He was avoiding the house and he pretended he could only snatch a few hours each time from his duty...The darkness of the room frightened him and he toyed with his hat...They sat in awkward silence until she asked him to draw up the blind...'It is only drawn because I found the light hard on my eyes. But what does it matter at this time? There will soon be a fill of darkness', she smiled. He handled the cord clumsily and it banged up. Even now, he thought bitterly, she was poeticizing; like the verses she wrote for religious magazines, like the dreamy graces that had always kept her distant from him. He saw her face in the first rush of harsh sunlight. Her brown eyes were as beautiful as ever and so wide and shining in the shrunken face. Then he bent his face again. She could see no reflection of herself as she watched the handsome bowed head of the man with tenderness. 'Marry again, Peter. Pick somebody who will try to understand you better than I did, and who would be good to the children. Try and keep them together'.[3]

So much of the tension and emotional complexity of the relationship is captured in these brief gestures, so much caught and held by images of light, the poetry of chiaroscuro reinforcing the inadequacy of ordinary language to express, or thought to conceptualize, the bewildering fact of her death. Here in these sentences is the voice of the mature McGahern, so mature in vision for a young man in his early twenties, his theme articulated: how to prepare for death, how to live with that knowledge. Elizabeth Reegan's inner monologue is heard here for the first time. The narrative style has moved entirely away from the feelings of the boy towards an adult way of seeing and thinking, which is not, however, a less dramatic way of feeling the unthinkable knowledge.

Yet the consciousness of Hugh in this chapter has dimensions it did not have in 'The Going', and his growing awareness of the fact of his mother's death ripples forward decades, almost unbelievably, as far as *Memoir*. One can only marvel at how the power of imagination, which dramatized the consciousness of the dying woman, is rooted in an intimacy with her feelings earlier, and that, as *Memoir* implies, McGahern's memory of those earliest times is actually the source of his imaginative power:

> The first primroses of the year appeared on a ditch over Brady's pond where the creamery horses drank. Hugh picked the flowers as he came from school and raced the rest of the way home. She was alone: the nurse was sleeping after a bad night; so he entered the darkened room without knocking. She woke out of a light sleep to welcome him joyfully. He stood at the door with his hands behind his back and refused to come nearer...A laugh of joy filled his throat and, running forward, he drew the primroses from behind his back. The five pale flowers made a pretty bunch in the boy's fingers. He held them to her face. She gave a small cry and tried to lift herself out of the pillows. 'Oh! They're lovely and so early', she whispered. He could hear her breathing in the rich perfume and letting it away again. A draft of wind lifted the blind and for a moment the window was streaked with rainy sunlight. It lit up the dust and small feathers on the bedclothes, but the flowers became a velvety yellow flame in the bones of her hand.

Such a vivid depiction of the boy's feelings, in darkness and light, focused now on the primroses and his sudden sense of the futility of his gesture in the face of the unnatural thing that is about to happen, is undoubtedly rooted in earliest memories. This scene in his first, unpublished, novel takes on an extraordinary charge when it is placed next to the closing lines of his final book, when he imagines his mother returning to visit him: 'If we could walk together through those summer lanes, with their banks of wild flowers that "cast a spell", we probably would not be able to speak...As we retraced our

steps, I would pick for her the wild orchid and the windflower.'4 So
many of these elements of the mother and son together in the landscape echo the scene of more than forty years before, and there can
be little doubt that McGahern's memory of his earliest years in the
Leitrim countryside is always an active force in his imaginative grasp
of the mystery of presence and loss, of mutability. In such ways, even
in this first novel, the intimate bond of memory and art can be felt.

Much of this novel does indeed seem to rely on recalled material—the family context, the violent and frustrated father who eventually remarries, the struggle with the promise to become a priest,
the sisters leaving home—and scenes are dramatized in a more
conventional, consecutive narrative of growing up than in *The Dark*
where so much of the same material is used. Certain scenes will
be revised and published in 1961, and these scenes will reappear,
rewritten, in *The Dark*. The core situations and experiences are also
familiar from *Memoir*. Among Hugh's experiences that are not
dramatized in *The Dark* or recalled in *Memoir* are the friendship with
Campbell and his relationship with Kathleen which occupies the
final chapters of the novel. These relationships were depicted as
formative ones at this point, in the late 1950s, but some years later
this material was stripped away as inessential, and *The Dark* focused
closely on the isolated consciousness of the adolescent. Later, in *The
Leavetaking*, what appears to be a version of the relationship with
Kathleen reappears in the early pages of Part II. There its significance is clearly marked: 'She named where she was from. The place
was in the heart of the mountains from where my mother had come.
I could see past the ballroom to the girl with the emery stone in the
hayfields on the side of those iron mountains. She had gone on a
similar scholarship to the same convent, to the same training college. It was the same beaten path a generation apart.'5 This briefly
recalled relationship which begins close to the end of the two years
in training college of Patrick Moran appears to echo 'that sweet
drunkenness of first infatuation' depicted at much greater length in
Hugh's relationship with the young teacher Kathleen. In all these
examples of recalled material, it is the use the material is put to that
matters, how intimately it adheres to the central idea of each novel,
to the stage of self-knowledge that is explored or needs to be explored to arrive at the deepest feelings.

The feelings of the adolescent Hugh in the relationship with Kathleen are, it seems, less necessary in the search for self-knowledge which all these fictions reflect. That may be the reason why it is not retained to any extent later and may even be a reason why the novel was abandoned. Although there is no overt Oedipal triangle in 'The End or the Beginning of Love', nor a direct signalling, as in *The Leavetaking*, that the attraction to the first girlfriend may be shadowed by feelings for the mother, the treatment of the relationship draws on a classic novel of such a situation, D. H. Lawrence's *Sons and Lovers*. In that novel, Paul Morel, loving his mother, who is depicted as the victim of the father, is trapped between his bond with the mother and his attraction to Miriam. McGahern appears to have read the novel in that phase of his reading in St Pat's when he felt the need to catch up with the classic modern writers whom he had not known earlier. He refers to Lawrence in that context and praises the novel later; passages of description of the mother and of the work in the fields echo Lawrence's novel, suggesting that it may have been in his mind also in the imagining of the relationship. It is predictable and novelettish, while the description of haymaking in the scene that follows its end appears vivid and natural; all the details of the scene—the men at work, the hare, the pigeon—suggest that the writer is more comfortable with this material. The ease of this writing foreshadows many scenes of manual work in McGahern's later fiction, including the extraordinary haymaking scene in *Amongst Women*, which seem to ground the characters in a natural rhythm, free of self-consciousness and tension.

The extended narrative of this young love between Hugh and Kathleen is McGahern's first treatment of a significant extra-familial relationship, and it is striking that he suppressed this novel, whether it was because it was too close to autobiography, as he suggested, or for other stylistic reasons, such as a new and conscious embracing of modernism. His abandonment of the story of Hugh and Kathleen seems to mark a realization about his own talent and how it would be developed. Although the *éducation sentimentale* of some of his characters interests him, the central thrust of his fiction—unlike that of Lawrence—explores family relationships. In the first half of his career, sexual relationships engage his interest, but gradually familial and communal bonds take precedence and the relationship of an individual consciousness to what he later called 'the natural process of living'.

While the young lovers part in frustration and rancour, Hugh does not find any more satisfaction in his religious faith and the vocation for the priesthood. By the end of the novel, unsurprisingly in a work of Irish fiction, he has given up on both and leaves for England: 'Why should he allow the living death of the priesthood to cheat him out of his right to live, the right to fashion his soul's life by his own thought?...he must live his own life with honesty and face whatever hell or heaven or nothingness that was beyond it on how he had lived it, and on that alone'. These thoughts situate Hugh in a well-written Irish tradition of revolt, and even of exile, even if they do not quite echo the stirring declarations of Stephen Dedalus that he will use 'silence, exile and cunning' as weapons that will enable him to forge the 'uncreated conscience of his race'. At no point in the novel does McGahern suggest to the reader that it is a 'portrait of the artist' or that Hugh's going into exile has a high-minded artistic motivation; rather, his going is emigration, an effort to escape from the desolation of his childhood, 'its loneliness and fears, his father's cruelty', and, like so many other young men, to find work.

The various layers of self-conquest in the novel may be elaborated further as McGahern's first effort to create an image of his life and of the culture that had shaped him. It is not part of McGahern's concern to analyse his community from a post-colonial perspective, yet in this first novel there is sympathy for his protagonist which comes from such a concern. Hugh fails to get a university scholarship and so, in spite of his talent, he cannot pursue higher education; neither can he be dependent on his father for support. He works with him on the farm, enjoys for a time the companionship of local people, but deep down he knows that he must claim his own life, away from repression and impoverishment. Hugh recognizes that his father feels abandoned and desolate when he announces his decision to leave, and he scarcely has the will to act on his impulse:

Outside the night was warm and fresh. He knew that if Kathleen hadn't finished with him that he would never have had the strength to leave. Even now it was hard to go, with the smell of new hay from the meadows, and the mist wondrous about the rusty, corrugated iron over the hayshed. He had always taken these things for granted...Up on the Plains of Boyle a few lights made a ghostly illuminated veil in the mist. Lamps shone through two windows on the slopes of Ballyfermoyle. There was little life on these hills, or in the village between them.

McGahern does not intensify the devastating vision of sterility and impotence which Patrick Kavanagh created in *The Great Hunger*, but the composite image which the narrative creates—the death of the mother, the frustration and violence of the father, the fear, the repressive Catholicism—is not only a personal experience; it is also a cultural paradigm of a form of death in life. Although Hugh is torn about leaving, the country people reinforce his aspiration: 'They wondered that he didn't make more use of his "fine schoolin'"' and go away to the big cities to find his place in the world.' Underlying such statements is an assumption that reflects a practical recognition of the time: the society that emerged from the War of Independence was an economic disaster and young people were growing up into a culture with a pervasive sense of failure and inferiority. Emigration seemed to be the necessary solution for many, since only by leaving could they find a livelihood and win self-esteem. Torn between harsh personal disillusionment and a recognition of the economic collapse which is denuding the countryside, Hugh tries to assert a kind of poise: 'He felt himself at a living moment in his life...His peace was perfect. He had no envy or hatred in him.'

While the narrative development in 'The End or the Beginning of Love' seems to bring the protagonist to a point of clarification and conviction, and departure from Ireland, there are aspects that also point forward to *The Dark*, a more anguished and unresolved depiction of adolescent consciousness. Hugh's struggle with the promise to his mother that he will be a priest resemble scenes in *The Dark*. Left alone in the house of his cousin, a priest, Hugh feels bewildered and angry, humiliated and abused:

A dull pain throbbed behind his eyes; he rested his forehead in desperation against the cold marble of the mantelpiece. His glance fell on the bulldogs snarling protection about the small statue and he laughed viciously: he wanted to smash them through the open window against a cross that rose over the border of laurel. 'The Irish people will never attain any sense of artistic order. How's this the old saying goes: "You can take the man out of the bog, but you can't take the bog out of the man", he mimicked and laughed a harsh grating laugh. He wanted to smash something.

The same idea appears briefly in *The Dark* where it is revealed that it is Father Gerald who says, more conventionally, 'Absolutely no sense of taste, a very uncultivated people even after forty years of freedom the mass of Irish are. You just can't make silk out of sow's ear at the drop of a hat.'[6] This unconventional priest unnerves the adolescent, but in both of these snobbish declarations he poses a challenge to the adolescent's sense of inferiority, which the young man sets out to conquer, in *The Dark* through higher education, and in 'The End or Beginning of Love' by leaving for England and thereby asserting his own freedom.

These scenes contribute to the understanding of the protagonist's intense frustration and need to break out, but the notions of attaining a 'sense of artistic order' or of cultivated 'taste' seem to stand beyond the narrative as another kind of attainment that the culture does not allow, or, at least, this is the challenge the priest seems to set before him. The condescending assumption that he will never be capable of recreating himself, that he will forever be a man of 'the bog', or a 'sow's ear' rather than 'silk', enrages the adolescent and his anger comes out as bitter mockery. The novel does not, in fact, investigate why 'the Irish people' will never attain 'artistic order', or, indeed what this aristocratic-sounding notion might mean, but it is surely something the young McGahern reflected on: what was his attitude to his cultural inheritance, to 'the bog'? Would his inheritance forever prevent him from attaining 'artistic order'?

It could be said that McGahern spent his whole career answering these questions, and disproving in different ways what the priest asserted. Like Kavanagh, who exemplified a countryman of limited education transforming himself into a poet of 'the bog', and then of the city, McGahern tried in various ways to combine the delicate lyrical mode, the 'silk', as it were, with the crude matter of the earth, and of those who lived close to it, as it were, the 'sow's ear'. After all, McGahern's excitement in early 1956 was for a poem such as 'Kerr's Ass' in which Kavanagh declared: 'I name their several names / Until a world comes to life— / Morning, the silent bog, / And the god of imagination waking / In a Mucker fog.'[7] It might be an exaggeration to say that *Tarry Flynn* is a submerged presence in this novel of youth in the country, and that the 'peace' Hugh suddenly aspires to is Kavanagh's newly found peace in the 1950s: 'Gather the bits of road that were / Not gravel to the traveller / But eternal lanes of joy / On which no man who walks can die.'[8] At any rate, it seems that this first novel embodies an attempt to come to terms with issues that were not simply adolescent ones; it looks forward to a long career in which McGahern would search through material not essentially different for his own 'artistic order'. He will search for a distinctive style by embracing both the classic literature of Europe and his difficult local inheritance, both in their different ways avenues to a 'vision of reality'. By the end of his life, he will have turned aside many times to celebrate Gloria Bog.

8

'The abiding life'

Beginning in August 1959, 'The End or the Beginning of Love' was sent out to various publishers in London. Patrick Swift also saw it, and he and David Wright, editors of a new publication, *X: A Quarterly Review of Literature and the Arts*, expressed an interest in publishing a number of extracts. Between August 1959 and the summer of 1960, McGahern waited for publishers' reactions to his first novel and worked on short fiction, but, more importantly, this is the period when the groundwork for *The Barracks* was laid. After the school year ended, he settled into a reading of all Tolstoy's fiction, at the suggestion, earlier, of Michael McLaverty. In August, he writes that *War and Peace* is a great novel, comparing it to Thomas Mann's *The Magic Mountain*, and he compares a story, 'My Husband and I', to passages in *Remembrance of Things Past*. But 'The Death of Ivan Ilyich' had evoked a reaction deeper than literary criticism: 'I was working at the time I read "Ivan"; it so excited me that I had to put it away until I was finished.'[1] That excitement appears to be what triggered the 'reading through his novels', and, again, 'Ivan', which he thought 'a far greater story than Joyce's "The Dead", though not unlike it'. Of course, that story of how intimately the present may be haunted by an earlier death is not the only story in *Dubliners* that evokes a moribund state, a death-in-life, which is Joyce's subject, nor is its style irrelevant to the work McGahern is about to undertake.

A later remark on the style of *Dubliners* has a striking relevance to 'A Barrack Evening', the working title of the new novel: 'The prose never draws attention to itself except at the end of "The Dead", and by then it has been earned: throughout, it enters our imaginations as stealthily as the evening invading the avenue in "Eveline".'[2] It is an extraordinarily revealing statement on how style 'enters our imaginations'—how, in fact, the silent and stealthy passage of time

towards the evenings of life is mirrored in a language that mesmer-
izes by its lack of demonstrativeness. The sentences mirror life in
their registering of how death happens over time, inevitably, and
whatever the actual circumstances; the fact of death and the passage
of time towards that end are the experiences McGahern will dramatize in the new novel, and it is in this way that 'representations of
particular lives' will capture 'all of life'. While theme and structure
may echo 'The Death of Ivan Ilyich', undoubtedly a revelatory story
on the way to the writer's conceiving of the dying of Elizabeth
Reegan, the style certainly owes a great deal to Joyce's early work:
'Joyce does not judge...Material and form are inseparable.' The
style will reflect the life of Elizabeth, the plot simply following the
last months of her life, and the evenness of tone will allow for the
subtle shadings of her dramatic inner registering of the passage of
time.

   In fact, this period from summer 1959 to the summer of 1961
marks for John McGahern the decisive step out of apprenticeship
and into the identity of a classic novelist. The correspondence with
Michael McLaverty suggests a number of stages in this process, the
first being this discovery of Tolstoy. At the end of February 1960,
before they met for the first time, McGahern sent McLaverty part
of 'The End or the Beginning of Love', but already he had begun
to distance himself from it: 'I brought very little away of the work as
I conceived it. It grows very little in my eyes in the past few months.'[3]
He is ready for McLaverty to be 'painfully just' in his response and
confesses that when they met he was 'overjoyed' at his sense of
McLaverty's integrity. Their bond at this time, and until *The Dark*
appeared in 1965, expressed itself in a shared critical vocabulary of
truth and honesty for judging fiction, and by these criteria, few Irish
writers measured up to what they had found in Chekhov and Tolstoy. It was, of course, the conception and the writing of the new
novel that focused his confidence regarding style and the judgement
of other writers, and that is what is indirectly revealed in so many
of his letters to McLaverty and others during these years. While he
greatly trusted McLaverty's judgement, McGahern was also capable
of expressing sharp differences of opinion about particular texts or
writers, and, clearly, felt the need to do so to preserve his own
integrity.

A letter of 1961 clarifies this matter in terms that reveal the depth of McGahern's own commitment to a vision of life that *The Barracks* first embodies. He writes to McLaverty about a story they have read in the *New Yorker*:

> I found the story a coarse exposition of human longing, vulgar, and the writing leaden with statement. The people for me had no reality or *dignity*, they were not seen with any vision, or in the pity of their passing lives. As often in the pages of the *New Yorker* I found she was superior or at least indifferent to these people, something a human being cannot be, and definitely not an artist, for are we not all accused together in our nature? I think your own work is the very antithesis of this story.[4]

A year earlier, he had written: 'It is difficult to reconcile the desire to do nothing but write...with all the human suffering about us.'[5] The seriousness of purpose, the absolute need to make art justify itself, to root it in a depth of feeling and a vision of the reality of life express a Tolstoyan ambition. In these terms, and fortified by McLaverty's clarity of purpose and quiet integrity, it is clear that the art of fiction McGahern has begun to practise draws on his whole self to a degree not realized earlier.

While McGahern's reading in these years included novels with a large and panoramic scope—*Remembrance of Things Past, The Magic Mountain,* and *War and Peace*—it is notable that his own work will consist of short stories and novels that in many ways are like extended novellas. As a writer of fiction, he had no interest in the large-scale narrative architecture or historical reconstructions of Proust, Mann, or Tolstoy. The literature he admired and the writers he imitated or learned a method from are not a homogeneous group, nor necessarily the same writers, nor are their most monumental works the part of their achievement that allowed him to gain access to the vision and style to which he responded most deeply. In the case of Joyce, for instance, it was *Dubliners* that engaged him more than *A Portrait of the Artist as a Young Man* or *Ulysses*, and certainly *Finnegans Wake* not at all. In the case of Tolstoy, as in the others, it appears that he immersed himself in a wide range of writings, 'novels, autobiographies and stories', captured, it seems, by

Tolstoy's preoccupation with death and the search for meaning in moral and spiritual terms.

It may be that 'The Death of Ivan Ilyich' left him in a state of 'excitement' on first reading, as he reports to McLaverty, but the protagonist's response to the realization that in middle age he is about to die is scarcely unique in Tolstoy's work. The grotesque unreality of daily routines, ambitions, and well-meaning gestures, which is unveiled as Ivan Ilyich struggles in anger and despair to find meaning in the fact of his own mortality, is not so different from the horrific absurdities of the Napoleonic campaigns which are detailed in *War and Peace*. The wish for spiritual enlightenment and moral purpose, explored in brief in the novella, is a reflection of the large-scale and lengthy search of Pierre Bezuhov or, in *Resurrection*, of Prince Nekhludov. In fact, that quest for meaning, central to so many of these works and counterpointed with the absurd slaughter of individuals in war or the suffering they endure in prison, comes to a focus for McGahern in the smaller fictions of death and dying, or perhaps in passages or episodes of the larger works.

For instance, it is hard not to believe that certain chapters in Book Four of *War and Peace* brought McGahern to the heart of Tolstoy's vision in ways that affected the writing of *The Barracks* and had a lasting impact on his entire career. After years of searching for enlightenment, Pierre finds himself a prisoner of the French forces as they withdraw from Moscow. Apparently sentenced to be executed, he waits his turn as those ahead of him are killed, one by one, at close quarters, as he looks on from his place in the line. His first thoughts are that an impersonal and absurd coincidence of circumstances is the power that will end his life, all the players in this drama conspiring with the inevitable. With 'curiosity and agitation' he watches the young man who 'like a wounded wild beast looked around him with glittering eyes'. Suddenly, the sequence of executions ends, and as the horror of it sinks in on Pierre and on the soldier-executioners, he sees the bodies in a pit and has a passing glimpse of one of the bodies still alive before it is submerged under shovelfuls of earth:

> From the moment Pierre had witnessed that hideous massacre committed by men who had no desire to do it, it was as if the

spring in his soul, by which everything was held together and given the semblance of life, had been suddenly wrenched out, and all had collapsed into a heap of senseless refuse. Though he did not realize it, his faith in the right ordering of the universe, in humanity, in his own self and in God had been destroyed...
He felt that to get back to faith in life was not in his power.[6]

In fact, that faith is soon rekindled by the presence of a fellow-prisoner, Platon Karateyev, whose calm demeanour and simplest gestures of kindness become for Pierre emblematic of a way of life far removed from the violence and horror that surround them. He notes Karateyev's qualities of character, 'unusual hardiness and endurance', 'an unfathomable, rounded-off, eternal personification of the spirit of simplicity and truth', an ability to feel in sympathy with 'every creature with whom life brought him into contact'. Pierre, we are told, will preserve 'a most vivid and precious memory' of this man, whose 'words and actions flowed from him as smoothly, as inevitably and spontaneously as fragrance exhales from a flower'. These last words are associated by Tolstoy with an ideal Russian peasant, but for McGahern they must surely echo the 'moral fragrance' that he had found in Forrest Reid's book on Yeats and which he associated with Proust's spire and the spiritual purpose of art. A feeling of 'moral alertness' comes to possess Pierre as, inspired by Karateyev, he experiences a 'perfect happiness' in conditions of deprivation and scarcity: 'Those dreadful moments of anguish he had gone through at the executions had, as it were, washed for ever from his imagination and his memory the restless ideas and feelings that had formerly seemed so important.'[7] In these most extreme circumstances of desolation and impersonal violence, Tolstoy imagines a vision of serenity and natural goodness.

Inserted between these chapters that focus on Pierre, however, is a set of chapters which describe the death of Prince Andrei in domestic circumstances. Wounded in the war, he is brought to the Rostovs' temporary home since they have fled from Moscow, where Natasha cares for him in his last days. His sister Maria travels in perilous circumstances to see him, but these two most caring and solicitous women are excluded from his inner life as he faces his own mortality:

His speech, his voice, and especially that calm, almost antagonistic, look betrayed the detachment from all earthly things
which is so terrible for a living man to witness. He plainly
found it difficult to understand the concerns of this world; yet
at the same time one felt that he failed to understand, not
because he had lost the power of understanding but because
he understood something else—something the living did not
and could not understand, and that entirely absorbed him.[8]

The separation of the dying person from the circumambient world
of things and people, even those most intimate in love, is remarkable, and in this case, unlike that of Ivan Ilyich, the feelings of Andrei
are marked by 'a strange and joyous lightness in his being' and a
freedom from fear as he becomes aware of a 'principle of eternal
love'. This inner life is unknown and unknowable, the narrator insists, to the two women: 'they wept from the emotion and awe
which took possession of their souls before the simple and solemn
mystery of death that had been accomplished before their eyes'.[9]
Tolstoy's belief in an eternal life beyond the 'mystery' of death is
affirmed as a reality which cannot be known or understood by
human reason; in this sense, the final stages of Elizabeth Reegan's
death in *The Barracks* are anticipated more clearly than in the dying
of Ivan Ilyich.

    While Tolstoy's vision is revealed in its essential elements in these
chapters of *War and Peace*, a much shorter work, his very first fiction,
includes a passage which bears a striking resemblance to material
even more intimately resonant for the author of 'The Going' and
'The End or the Beginning of Love'. This work is 'Childhood', an
autobiographical fiction that culminates in the deathbed scene of a
boy and his mother. Tolstoy's father and mother had in fact died
when he was in his first years, so that the scenes of the boy's relationship with his mother and then his presence at her deathbed are
fictional, even though in other elements the narrative appears to be
close to autobiography. At the outset, the narrator confides:

So many memories of the past arise when one tries to recall
the features of someone we love that one sees those features
dimly through the memories, as though through tears. They
are the tears of imagination. When I try to recall my mother

as she was at that time I can only picture her brown eyes which always held the same expression of goodness and love... but the complete image escapes me.[10]

Readers of McGahern's manifesto, 'The Image', in which he speaks of the struggle of the artist to recover 'the image on which our whole life took its most complete expression once', or of his final narrative of his undiminished love for his mother in *Memoir*, may feel the presence of Tolstoy, who in such ways may have merged for McGahern with Proust.[11]

But it is at the end of 'Childhood', during the deathbed scenes, that there is an eerie feeling that 'The Going' and this narrative are kindred texts: 'I was in great distress at this moment, yet I automatically noticed every little detail. It was almost dark in the room, and very hot... The smell struck me so forcibly that, not only when I happen to smell it but when I even recall it, my imagination instantly carries me back to that dark stifling room and reproduces every minute detail of that terrible moment.'[12] The horror of his mother's dead body and his days of grief are depicted in detail, and if he is overwhelmed by the emotion of the days, he is struck by the 'affront to her memory' of the resumption of 'the ordinary course of life'. But then his parting from 'the person I loved most in the world' is alleviated by a recognition: 'Only people capable of loving deeply can experience profound grief; but the very necessity they feel to love serves as an antidote to grief and heals them. That is why the human spirit is more tenacious of life than the body.'[13] In these words, it may be that McGahern found the seed of *The Leavetaking*, the fiction which will incorporate 'The Going' and the protagonist's recovery from his grief. And Tolstoy's narrator recognizes too that, even more than himself, his mother's old and loyal serving woman has loved her, and in the final chapter of 'Childhood', he imagines the serving woman's death: 'She accomplished the best and greatest thing in life—she died without regret or fear.'[14] Just as the peasant Platon had inspired a faith in life in Pierre, this simple woman provides the narrator with an inspiration for life. The final line of the novella, 'Can Providence really have united me with these two beings only in order that I should for ever mourn their loss?', is not only a mark of Tolstoy's lifelong search for the appropriate vision of life in the face of death, it is surely an inspiration for the career of the young novelist whose deepest feelings were rooted in such an experience.

McGahern's discovery that Tolstoy's work could affect him deeply and become a touchstone of his imaginative development at this stage is not entirely surprising, even though it may appear at first out of line with his developed interest in the modernist Proust and the post-modernist Beckett. In fact, the ways in which he was capable of finding what he needed in many different European and Irish writers, the ways in which he clarified his own style through independent recall or silent absorption of Russian or other writers, is a measure of his talent and his accomplishment in later decades. Just as with Yeats or Proust, or other classic writers, he appears to have thrown himself completely into gaining a comprehensive sense of Tolstoy's achievement, and it may be that in this period, 1959–60, his awakening to the Russian's vision, and his recognition of how it had been appreciated by McLaverty and other Irish writers, moderated the impact of Proust and Beckett on the kind of fictional realism he embraced in writing *The Barracks*. A decade later when he began to adapt Tolstoy's play *The Power of Darkness*, he remarked that 'most of Tolstoy's fiction was by then part of my mind'.[15]

The interest of Patrick Swift and David Wright in publishing episodes from 'The End or the Beginning of Love' prompted McGahern to go to London for an extended stay in the summer of 1960. McGahern wrote a vivid account of that visit in an affectionate essay in celebration of Patrick Swift. 'The Bird Swift', evokes the excitement of the young writer in London artistic circles at this time, but it is also measured through mature reflection, and the trajectory the novelist followed into *The Barracks* and in following years can be detected.

From the beginning of his career, Swift had been as much a writer as a painter, a writer about art, that is, although he disliked the notion of being an art critic, and his ideas about the character of the artist were as often based on literary figures as on painters. His contributions to *Envoy*, between 1949 and 1951, included appreciations of the artist Nano Reid and more general questions of modern art appreciation, but his interest in Auden's poetry, which he quoted frequently, and in the poetry of Kavanagh were equally significant. And when he wrote for *X*, he wrote on the poet George Barker, as well as on such topics as 'Art and Morality', 'The Painter in the Press', and 'Mob Morals and the Art of Loving Art'. His essays are fluent and argumentative, with frequent allusions to literature. It is worth noting that they include references to Beckett's essay on Proust, to Stendhal's writing on Italian painting, to Baudelaire on art, and Remy de Gourmont on beauty, and the underlying argument may be detected here: 'Art, profound and original, created in solitude and in anguish by men outside and ahead of their time is something we can now conceive of and be prepared to look for.'[16] It is a statement that refers to himself, to Kavanagh, and to painters he admires. Equally striking, and pertinent to McGahern, is his comment on his favourite Dutch painter: 'The suffering, ignominy and death of Rembrandt...has about it an archetypal quality. It is the case of a man triumphant over terrible circumstances through the exercise of his art.'[17] And his comment 'the prototypical great painter, it may be, bears a closer resemblance to John Constable than to Sir Joshua Reynolds' points to McGahern's discovery of his admiration not only of paintings by Constable (which Swift took McGahern to see), or his character, but his letters too. In the excitement of London, in the middle of the avant-garde art scene—there are references to Picasso, Francis Bacon, and Lucian Freud—it is surely significant that McGahern would admire most Constable's paintings and his letters, and indeed find in the lives of the Romantic landscape artist and the Dutch portrait painter exemplary figures.

It is evident that McGahern consulted the essays from *X* before he wrote his appreciation, and he concludes that Swift did not have 'a natural feeling for language': 'What interested him was ideas and the conflict of ideas and their power when seen throught the fascination of a powerful personality.'[18] It might also be said that what interested Swift was the revelation of character and the inner life in art, and so his interest in portrait-painting and his insistence on the search for the unique vision are of more fundamental importance, something McGahern detected behind all the talk and which he appreciated in Swift. In the end, they seemed to agree on fundamentals. '"You can't write about painting," he asserted. "The whole thing is tactile. The canvas is either alive or it isn't. You can only look".'[19] On their visits to the various galleries, McGahern came to feel that he could not see paintings as Swift could see them: 'I could never feel or see through paint the way I could with words.' McGahern declares he did not possess 'a strong natural visual talent', and these distinctions are remarkable for their emphasis on 'natural feeling' and 'natural talent', as if the gifts of character are more important than anything learned. They can talk about Proust, as they did, and Stendhal, and 'the great passage on memory in St Augustine's *Confessions*', but the essay concludes with a quotation from St Thomas Aquinas, which Swift includes in one of his essays: 'The image is a principle of our knowledge.' This much McGahern entirely agrees with, and he will often return to that fundamental starting point: that all art 'centres on bringing the clean image that moves us out into the light'.[20] His interest in Swift's painting and in all painting that he could appreciate is focused here on the image of one's spiritual life that only the best artists can bring into the light.

This is how McGahern explained the goal of his own work from this point on, and here is the explanation for his poetic approach to the self, an approach that analytical writing cannot equal, whether critical or biographical; in noting that Swift disliked George Painter's biography of Proust and Richard Ellmann's biography of Joyce (both published to acclaim the previous year), he summed up sympathetically Swift's post-Catholic conviction: 'the abiding life is always in the private world of the spirit'. Yet there is a crucial difference between them: '"It would be obscene to be anything but a romantic in this conformist age," Paddy asserted, and I disagreed, thinking it was more a matter of temperament and background.'[21]

The warmth of the friendship as it is recalled in McGahern's memoir-essay, and as it can be seen in contemporary letters, may include McGahern's feelings towards the whole Swift family. In fact, this is where his recollection begins, discounting Swift's reputation in the bars around Grafton Street and evoking the family he got to know in the mid-1950s. 'In the small house on Carrick Terrace, which was suffused with the mother's extraordinary energy and charm, I saw [Patrick's] drawings and paintings for the first time— I remember with particular vividness a small watercolour of a Rialto sweetshop.' And when they visited together the National Gallery in London, in July, McGahern recalls that Patrick always went to the

Rembrandt Room: ' "It's all so simple, such magic, so much life and death in one canvas," he said once. When I look at some of the portraits of his mother I am reminded of the portrait of Maria Trapp which he so much admired.'[22] At the end of McGahern's stay, Swift did a drawing of him to be taken back to Dublin for his mother. Certainly, there is a vivid portrait of Patrick in the essay, but while his circle in London, his articulated ideas on art, and his support of McGahern's first fiction were important, there is an implication that it was the Swift family in Dublin, perhaps even the mother, as well as the sons, who were of more lasting value to McGahern. Two years later when X closed down, Patrick, apparently disillusioned with the world of art and artists in London, left for an isolated country place in Portugal, where he remained for the rest of his life. McGahern may never have met him again, but later references by McGahern to the novelist Eça de Quieros suggest that Patrick remained a presence in the family, for this classic Portuguese novelist was a favourite of his, as can be seen in the books on the Algarve and Lisbon Swift wrote with David Wright. In the mid-1970s, after McGahern withdrew to his own isolated country place in County Leitrim, he too took a keen interest in the work of de Quieros.

When McGahern returned from London, he brought the gift of the drawing to the Swift family home. 'Your mother was so excited with the Drawing', he writes to Patrick; 'I never saw anyone so delighted.'[23] This follows a statement that he doesn't like writing letters: 'It is so easy to be anything except honest here.' And then, as if to exemplify his absolute commitment to honesty of expression and tact in recognizing the delicacy of intimate feeling, he declares: 'People dislike strangers speaking intimately about the ones they love.' He honours Patrick's love for his mother and, while not wanting to intrude, he seems to admit his own love for her.

Then he went down to Roscommon, to the house of his father and stepmother in Grevisk, which he refers to as 'home'. Curiously, he does not refer to his father or family in this letter to Swift, but he includes a rapturous description of the orchard and grounds of the Rockingham estate. It is an elegy for what it once was 'in its heyday, but they still talk about it round [here]'. The Georgian mansion had burned down in 1956, yet his letter creates a visual image for the painter: 'A few things like the belfry, several evergreens and a few walnut trees, wild mint or rose and thousands of narcissi in the pastures in Spring are all that tell now.' He writes at length of the fruit trees—apples and pears and plums, 'long wine-coloured Victorias'—regretting that Swift's daughters cannot be there to pick the fruit and regretting that 'I cannot bring you there.' In a letter that speaks of the importance of honesty in letter-writing, the long description conveys great feeling, perhaps a Constable-like attachment to the scene, a reattachment to the landscape itself: 'I used to go down the long sheep paddocks of the Demesne nearly every morning to the spring river—for drinking water.'

But if the letter includes such intimate images of deep attachment to the place, and he ends by confessing how much he enjoyed the time with Swift, 'I'll never forget it', this communication of early September 1960 is revealing of another side of the young writer. Between the lines, a determined and clear new direction is being mapped out, the path that will take him to *The Barracks*. While this and other letters discuss the passages from 'The End or the Beginning of Love' which have been accepted for publication in *X*, it is clear that they have been discussing the novel as a whole and how publishers have been reacting to it. He has been receiving rejection slips, and has begun to doubt his achievement in the first novel. Swift is his confidant. He did spend time rewriting the passages that Swift wanted to include in *X*, but, energized by his time spent in London, he has plans. Already, he tells him, 'I've started tricking with the novel, and I'll soon be working. There'll be two this time. Then I'll be able to get on out of it for good.' It would seem that these references are to the material of his mother's death and of his adolescence with his father, the basic material of 'The End or the Beginning of Love', which he wishes to put behind him; his plan for doing so is to write two novels, 'two this time', presumably what will become *The Barracks* and *The Dark*. By separating the material in two, he is sure that he can move beyond his apprenticeship: 'I'll work it out so much better. It'll be a real, real work then: and they can say what they want to about it.'

While this plan, articulated in September 1960, is significant, his reaction to the publishers' rejections of his first novel is equally significant for it focuses on the issue of how to transform autobiographical experience into fiction:

The insistence that to string a few lunatic situations into a plot is more valuable and difficult than to give passion and pattern to the lives of people being eroded out of existence in the banality and repetitiveness of themselves and their society is the real maddening thing. I better leave it so! But the autobiographical stunt! Very few of the situations in the book ever happened in my life—in that sense, it is no more mine than the Man in the Moon's autobiography. THE WHOLE BOOK owes everything to my experience, the way I suffered and was made to laugh, the people I have lived among, the landscape and the books I liked,—in that way it is as auto. as I am capable of making it. But it is seldom possible to be ourselves in real life: because of the need FOR MONEY, for friends, sex, a beloved, or even, I suspect, because of the need to have enemies. And if you feel you must be a responsible individual in some manner, and can't, or do not wish, or feel that it's not enough to be a saint, then you have little choice but to try some artifice. The common notion that you can make an art out of your life, refinements of pleasure, etc, is pure moonshine as far as I see it. There must be some morality.

This remarkable letter is prompted by many impulses, and because he felt that Swift was receptive and, indeed, because he wanted Swift on his side, he is more forthcoming about his tangle of feelings than he might otherwise be. It appears that he has been angered by a publisher's wish for more plotting and by a comment that the novel is autobiographical. While denying that most of the 'situations' are autobiographical, he insists that 'the whole book' is autobiographical; in short, that in the most fundamental sense the individual style of a work of art draws on everything the artist has experienced and known.

But he goes on to say that the morality of the book inheres in its artifice rather than in its literal reproduction of personal experience. And he insists that artifice is also necessary for life, an idea that appears to echo the Yeatsian notion of the mask, but, always practical, McGahern grounds it in the various needs of the individual. Also striking in the letter is the insistence on the difficulty of giving 'passion and pattern' to a vision of life which is inescapably banal and repetitive. Here the Proustian and Beckettian paradigm becomes evident which will in time become the heart of *The Barracks*. The confident rejection of the superficial requirements of publishers ends with a ringing declaration: 'While there's the need to be a responsible individual and you don't turn to [be a] saint, it seems to me that the need to be an artist must remain, a whole life long. And that's a hell of a long way from writing autobiography.' The search which the artist undertakes, he seems to be saying, is a lifelong search for the 'passion and pattern' which will redeem a life 'being eroded out of existence'. The terms of this commitment are religious, analogous to sainthood, and also moral, and while they may reflect in part what he has heard from Swift in relation to Rembrandt, Constable, or Cézanne, these words are unmistakably the words of McGahern as he clarifies the lifelong journey on which he has embarked.

Michael McLaverty's physical distance from Dublin and its various literary figures allowed for a freedom and independence in his judgement of fiction, and this in turn seems to have encouraged McGahern to share with him his immediate response to what he read. In their first letters, Kavanagh and O'Faolain had been assessed, the latter failing to win any respect from McGahern. Frank O'Connor, the other writer of short stories whose success was at its peak in the United States in the early 1960s, is referred to briefly, but few of his stories had appealed to McLaverty, who early on mentioned a recent story, 'The New Teacher', which he found 'so silly, so palpably unreal I often wonder why he enclosed it between the covers of a book'. McGahern's silence in this case and throughout the correspondence is clearly a reflection of disinterest, and he is firm in his conclusion: 'of living Irish prose writers I admire your works most'.[24]

McLaverty had a high opinion of one Irish writer, and after recommending her stories to McGahern, he urged him to contact her. This is Mary Lavin, a professional writer whose work appeared regularly in the *New Yorker*; she was also a devoted single mother (widowed since 1954). She was friendly with Roger McHugh, Frank O'Connor, and other established figures, but in these years she opened her home and offered stimulating intellectual conversation late into the night to aspiring writers, many of them students from UCD. Tom Kilroy, Nuala O'Faolain, Augustine Martin, Paul

Durcan, Tom MacIntyre were among those who were regulars at her mews in Ladd Lane, a short distance from the university. Her maternal and gregarious personality offered a different kind of emotional and intellectual climate from the male pub culture, and, through her American background and success, to a different kind of literary life. McLavery had been urging McGahern for some time to make contact with her before he eventually did in early 1960.

He reported to McLaverty, 'she received me with great kindness. I think she is the most charming and interesting woman I ever met.' Lavin has been characterized as an intense conversationalist whose attention to each person made them feel that she considered them uniquely interesting. Apart from that, her literary interests caught McGahern's attention: 'I also found that our vision of life and writing had much in common and that—deplore it how we may—is the most exciting discovery of all.'[25] Tom Kilroy has remarked that 'Mary Lavin is one of a generation of Irish writers who looked in the most natural fashion imaginable to the great European canon for examples to write by.' He recalled receiving copies from her in the early 1960s of Turgenev's novels and Tolstoy's 'The Kreutzer Sonata', as well as Flaubert's *Trois Contes* and remembered her talking about the death of Félicité in *Un cœur simple*. She gave him 'an education in books', he concluded.[26] While McGahern's reading already included much work by the great nineteenth-century French and Russian authors, the passion of her commitment, recalled here in Kilroy's note on his own awakening, must have reinforced McGahern's conviction and judgement, as his contact with McLaverty was also doing.

McLavery was aware of unevenness in Lavin's work but had been a long-time admirer of stories that he now encouraged McGahern to read. A decade earlier, he had praised her work in terms that seem to identify the 'vision' that appealed to him and to McGahern:

> They are true and will remain true for at no time do we feel that there is falsification or romanticizing of the material... what delights me above all in her work is the way she can capture mood by the rhythm of her language. Some modern stories give the impression they were written by a pneumatic

drill but hers have ease, urbanity, growth, and inevitability. Rhythm in language is disappearing from English prose style and the defect is due to the want of total immersion in the theme so that the resultant mood engendered can gather round itself the rhythm necessary for its total expression.[27]

In such critical terms, the early bond of McGahern to McLaverty, and, initially, to Lavin, can be glimpsed, and there are echoes of McGahern's own critical vocabulary in later years.

How regularly he went to the mews on Ladd Lane in these years is not clear, probably not often, but he did remain within Lavin's circle through mutual friendships. Following another visit, in September 1960, he wrote to McLaverty that 'she is a charming person. She is sadly very busy, and always [has] crowds of people about her', a remark that suggests that he may feel marginalized by Mary Lavin's entourage. As early as mid-1961, he confessed to McLaverty, moreover, that he did not like her most recent collection of stories, *The Great Wave*, something that made him feel awkward about any further meetings. From this point on, he appears to have distanced himself, became critical of Mary Lavin's work, and, a decade later, wrote a story, 'Doorways', that includes a recognizable and unflattering portrait of her. Lavin was sufficiently committed to him and his work two years after they met, however, to recommend his first stories to her literary agent in New York, who set up a contact for McGahern with editors at the *New Yorker*.

While he may have found Lavin and the gatherings at her house socially difficult, McGahern's entrance into the domestic ambience of Lavin's life and work coincided with his own movement as a writer into a female world in imagining the consciousness of Elizabeth Reegan. In the years before *The Barracks*, there is not much evidence that McGahern consciously set about studying women's work—even though Lavin was a devotee of Jane Austen, Katherine Mansfield, and Eudora Welty, and McLaverty also favoured domestic and familial material in his fiction. It is important to note also that apart from novels like *The Barracks* and *Amongst Women*, anchored in domestic routine, McGahern appears to have been conscious that his natural material had a strongly male orientation. His new work needed a counterbalance of awareness and, perhaps, style that were informed by the writing of women.

Elizabeth Cullinan, an Irish-American, who had worked at the *New Yorker* since the mid-1950s, and whose stories began to appear there in 1960, arrived in Dublin in early 1961 and stayed for three years.[28] William Maxwell, fiction editor of the *New Yorker*, gave her an introduction to Mary Lavin, and it was through Lavin that McGahern came to know her. On the evidence of the letters to McLaverty, they seem to have spent a significant amount of time together. Cullinan, a year older than McGahern, was greatly impressed by his reading, and recalled many years later his knowledge of Proust's novel, essays, and letters; Yeats's essays; and the Russians—Tolstoy, Chekhov and Isaac Babel. She remembered that he already 'had a deep and coherent sense of the world'.[29] McGahern discussed Cullinan's stories with McLaverty, and those of another *New Yorker* writer known to her—Maeve Brennan, an exiled Dubliner—and in a general way, this talented American writer may have awakened his interest in the work of American writers of the short story, many of whom he will admire in future years. A story of the mid-1960s, 'A Swim', and a later novel, *A Change of Scene*, include portraits of a character who resembles the McGahern of these years, and it may be that Cullinan served as a model for the American girl in stories such as 'Doorways' and 'Bank Holiday'; but, whatever the style of the portraits, these fictions confirm that the time McGahern and Cullinan spent together constituted an important episode in the sentimental education of each of them.

He also met Nuala O'Faolain at Ladd Lane. Her memoir *Are You Somebody?* includes an account of a number of relationships in her student years covering her time close to McGahern. Early in the summer of 1962, she returned to Dublin from postgraduate studies at the University of Hull. Speaking of their dates at centre-city cinemas, and pubs around Clontarf and Fairview, she implicitly identifies herself as the model for the girl in 'Sierra Leone', and it is possible that McGahern's relationship with her also contributed to 'My Love, My Umbrella'. She singles out solitude as characteristic of the man, but the extracts from the letters she quotes imply his exasperation with her and his need for sincerity: 'The only world is the world of love, and if we're true we must be consumed in whatever reality there is. All the rest is silly business.'[30] While these words foreshadow the love relationship in *The Leavetaking*, and Matthew

Arnold's words quoted there, 'Let us be true to one another', a much more immediate presence is the desperate need of Elizabeth Reegan for a 'total love' founded on acceptance and praise. The man O'Faolain knew was the person who had just come through two years of writing *The Barracks*. In a newspaper column written at the time of McGahern's death, O'Faolain remarked that, in spite of their poverty, they were intellectually rich. She was surely acute in her observation that he had absorbed Rilke's advice in *Letters to a Young Poet*, a gift from him to her: 'that you may find in yourself enough patience to endure and enough simplicity to have faith; that you may gain more and more confidence in what is difficult and in your solitude among other people'.[31]

McGahern's first published work, 'Episodes from a Novel', appeared in the fifth issue of *X* in March 1961. To appear in the pages of this highly esteemed London review, next to work by Beckett, Giacometti, Kavanagh, and Pound, ensured that McGahern's work would be noticed. And it was, even before publication. Charles Monteith of Faber and Faber contacted him with an offer of publication for the complete novel. He responded by saying that another publisher had made an offer to publish it and that 'in the revising another novel evolved which owed nothing to the first'. This was the 'good luck' that initiated his career, although McGahern preferred to show him 'A Barrack Evening', the beginning of his new novel, rather than 'The End or the Beginning of Love'. Monteith was immediately enthusiastic and offered him a contract for the novel. The first novel was withdrawn and remained unpublished.[32]

Monteith discovered that McGahern had completed the opening chapter of 'A Barrack Evening' to such a degree of perfection that he insisted the young writer should enter for the AE Memorial Award. This was one of the most distinguished Irish awards for established artists, and the idea of an unpublished novelist being eligible was presumptuous indeed. McGahern often told the story of the agreement he came to with Monteith. Since the cost of providing five copies of the typescript was exorbitant, 'he'd pay the cost if I lost, and I'd have to pay the cost if I won'.[33] By June, he had about half the novel written, 40,000 words, and he believed 'I have more power than ever before.'

The signs are that he worked quickly over these months, with a fierce intensity and certainty of purpose, although in his mind it was 'slow and backbreaking'. Towards the end of the year, it became known that the AE Memorial Award committee was considering it when they asked for additional chapters, and by then he was almost finished, except for polishing. By that time, the news of his contract with Faber and Faber had spread. John Montague invited him to submit an excerpt from the novel in progress for *The Dolmen Miscellany of Irish Writing*. 'A Barrack Evening' appeared next to poems by Thomas Kinsella, a story by Brian Moore, and work by established writers of the younger generation. Roger McHugh also invited him to submit an extract for an issue of *Threshold*, and, further afield, an episode was accepted for the *Transatlantic Review*. Suddenly, in less than a year, the still incomplete and unpublished novel took on a life in the literary world, but its author, now and always, kept his equanimity and his single-minded concentration on the work of composition.

Letters to McLaverty continue to map the contours of his critical thinking about good writing. He responded to a story of McLaverty's, 'After Forty Years', in a way that casts light on *The Barracks*: 'The only thing that troubled me, and this may be totally personal, was...at the end of their life...neither seemed to have *learned* or *seen* anything.'[34] He disagreed with McLaverty's criticism of Melville's 'Bartleby the Scrivener': 'it seems to me a beautiful and shocking vision of all-is-vanity, and the last passage a pure poem'.[35] Most striking of all is his response to the autobiography of Edwin Muir:

[It] is often moving and beautiful, though to me lacking in integrity and consequently intensity too, what is uniqueness. What Yeats said about Wordsworth came back to me as I read: his poetry lacks excitement and grows old before him because of a clinging to an alien morality, a morality of life or society, not the morality that is created in the vision of the work. You can have perfection of the life or work, but not of both. Purity of heart is to will one thing...An artist accepts for me everything utterly and loves it, once he first accepts the

first sin in its absurdity as completely as the saint accepts life
as a VIA. To regret one thing is to regret everything.[36]

Such clarity in his own thinking about the rooting of the imagination in character, and about the ways in which the imagination is
undermined and kept from producing work of integrity and individual vision, is fundamental to the writer of *The Barracks* and of so
much that followed, indeed of a lifelong commitment to his *via* as
artist.

9

Writing *The Barracks*

McGahern said that the character of Elizabeth Reegan is 'a way of seeing', which suggests that, in his conception of her, he objectified his own artistic vision. The external characterization of the family in the barracks, the scenes and plotting, the realism of its invention of rural Irish life in the 1940s are all remarkably accomplished. The precise observation of a culture in a particular historical period is vivid and concrete, as is the observation of seasonal change in the round of a year. For McGahern himself, however, the incentive in writing the novel was not simply to recreate a world he had known intimately in Cootehall but to discover a vision of life through the eyes of a woman dying of cancer. The challenge was not only to immerse himself in Elizabeth's world so that he could dramatize the environment in which she was going to live out her last days and months; his identification with her would also dramatize her inner world in an impassioned and intimate way.

The intensity of that identification would come from creating an inner monologue that would be true to how a middle-aged woman might think and feel and at the same time would incorporate a young man's vision. In a Flaubertian, impersonal manner, he would dramatize the inner and outer life of a woman somewhat like his mother, but just as Flaubert remarked, '*Madame Bovary, c'est moi!*', McGahern might have said 'Elizabeth Reegan is me'. While he draws on the fact of his own mother's death from cancer, it is, in the end, more true to say that the movements of Elizabeth's inner life and her reflections outward to her world owe more to McGahern's own need to find a 'way of seeing' and to discover how to make that world real, even as it is dissolving. 'She couldn't ever hope to get any ordered vision on her life. Things were changing, going out of her control, grinding remorselessly forward with every passing moment.'[1] Her discovery of her medical condition reduces the daily chores of caring for a household and children to no more than a willed effort. 'She was existing far within the dead walls and gaping out in mute horror.'[2] No less than her husband, she is 'a caged animal'. 'She could see no purpose, no anything, and she could not go on blindly now and without needing answers and reasons as she could once.'[3] At first overcome with despair and bewilderment, she is, nevertheless, determined 'to stand her ground here at last',[4] and the act of looking, of envisioning, of finding light in a darkening world become the poetic constants of her vital life. The vision of the book, its style and its philosophical investigations, are of profound importance to the writer. It is not an irony to say that its writing was a matter of life and death for him; looking back over his career, he insisted he wrote only because he needed to, to satisfy a spiritual or aesthetic need.

His instinct for the elements of fiction, for character, action, and setting; for dialogue and description; for pacing and construction had been formed by his reading, by intense responses to those fictional worlds that had given him both pleasure and a sense of individual style. His years of absorbing the craft enabled him to make some judicious decisions: he set the action of the novel in the barracks and in the village of Cootehall, County Roscommon—not in Aughawillan, County Leitrim, where his mother had lived in her final years. He was capable of writing out of a vivid, indelible, recall of the environment of his youth, the house, the village, the church, and then the county town. His selection of resonant and absolutely convincing details was made easier for him because he stayed so close to what he knew. Thus he could keep his concentrated energy for what was crucially important: dramatizing the inner life, the search for meaning and belief, and the style in which the known world could be made to mirror it.

In a concrete sense, McGahern was searching for a new belief in his own earlier world that had been emptied of belief. The traditional Catholic rituals no longer offered comfort or vision. The evening rosary, for instance: 'murmurs and patterns and repetitions that had never assumed light of meaning, as dark as the earth they walked, as habitual as their days'.[5] Or Christmas:

To see the first Christmas and to follow it down to this moment, joined in her here and ending in her death, and yet the external reality would run on and on and on as the generations...who was she and what was it? Her thought could begin on anything for object and still it travelled always the same road of pain to the nowhere of herself, it was as far as anything seemed to go...the unknowable reality, God...met you with imponderable silence and could never be reduced to the nothingness of certain knowledge.[6]

And yet, in spite of this frightening emptiness at the heart of Elizabeth's familiar world, new meaning would be knowable and refined only in her everyday life, her individual life set off against that of her husband, Sergeant Reegan, and the daily life of the small community of the barracks.

His subject, he said, was 'boredom. It was really to examine an enclosed world that had very little purpose. You could call it an existential novel in that sense—through the eyes of a sensitive, intelligent and essentially religious woman, in the true sense of the word "religious".'[7] The novel would not uncover a belief in a codified dogma or a philosophical schema; it would enact a set of answers to the question 'How to live in the shadow of death?' The answers would not be statements; they would be experiences grounded in images and a certain style. The search for a fulfilling purpose or for an attitude that would give meaning to routine life takes on a poignant or, perhaps, frantic urgency when the person engaged in the search is a woman who knows she is dying, but it was surely also crucial for the young McGahern in the years leading up to the writing of the novel. Writing *The Barracks* cleared the decks, brought him back to fundamentals, and shaped his thinking about life and art definitively.[8]

Imagining the death of his mother would always lead down into his deepest feelings, and without that opening to those feelings and to clear thinking about their meaning 'good writing' could not happen. The motto of Flaubert, borrowed from Buffon, was a central motto of McGahern also, and it is easy to see how the daily drama of Elizabeth's life in the barracks is coloured by deep and sometimes hidden feelings. The fear of mortality, of the inscrutable

impact of night falling over and over until the final darkness, is felt
on an instinctive level, even by the children. Each private moment
vibrates with the presence and vulnerability of being, even as social
contacts and interactions mask that privacy, and often the same
moment is overshadowed by monotony and boredom, the absence
of any feeling of vital life. The cycles of feeling and need, of questioning and craving, of numbness and calm are punctuated by
extraordinary flights of insight and vision.

'We work in the same material, Beckett and I', he remarked with
specific reference to this novel.[9] The pain of non-being—dramatized
in *Waiting for Godot*, narrated in Beckett's post-war fictions, and ana-
lysed in the essay on Proust—is present on a philosophical level and
also in the grim comedy of banal dialogue. The sergeant and his
policemen, Elizabeth and their wives, the Reegans and their children, all struggle through clichéd conversation, filling in the absurd
hours in ways that reveal the unmistakable presence of Samuel
Beckett. 'Nothing short of a miracle would change any of their lives,
[the guard's] lives, his life and her life without purpose, and it
seemed as if it might never come.'[10] The grim irony in this remark
is that Sergeant Reegan has been listening all evening to the clichéd
chatter of Guards Mullins, Brennan, and Casey, waiting for them to
finally leave; while the brilliantly done conversation recalls Joyce's
'Grace', for instance, or 'Cyclops', it is also reminiscent of *Waiting for
Godot*, for neither arrival nor departure will effectively change their
condition of being trapped in time and routine, waiting.

But if routine and habit reduce everything to a frightening banality, they also provide comfort. It is the paradox set out in Beckett's
Proust. During her time in the hospital, Elizabeth reflects: 'She had
such ease and peace and sense of everything being cared for: no
fear, no worries, no hours of indecision; the same things were done
at the same times every day; her meals came without her lifting a
hand; nurses changed the tired sheets and they felt light and cool as
air. She was plagued by no gnawing to see some guiding purpose in
her days.'[11] But since no feeling is pure or lasts long in this universe,
the 'fabricated structure of safe passions' collapses and the pain of
being possesses her, and then she craves comfort once more: 'the
work had to go on, grinding, incessant, remorseless; breaking her
down to its own dead impersonality, but never quite, and how often

she had half-wished to be broken into the deadness of habit like most of the rest, it was perhaps the only escape'.[12] The 'never quite' in that sentence is in the spirit of Beckett's solitaries, consciousness never still, forever reflecting, remembering, dreaming, individuality constantly present in the nuances of sense and perception and in the nuances of expression itself.

Elizabeth is keenly aware of the workings of her own mind and imagination, and it would not be in character for her to think of her reflections as 'play' like Beckett's Malone, for instance. Yet there are some basic similarities. In the hospital, Elizabeth finds herself:

> watching cars on a mountain road to pass the time, and having such dreams, it was such a fantastic comedy, and when she'd grow tired of her own she could turn and watch the others play... What kind of entrance and departure would she herself make, Elizabeth thought and knew she'd escape none of the lunacy of living because she could sometimes see... She was able to smile with some of the purity of music. She was still and calm and surely this way she saw was a kind of human triumph, even though this mood, as all her moods, was soon to change.[13]

The 'human triumph' expressed in the metaphor of music is surely an echo of the concluding paragraph of *Proust*: 'Music is the catalytic element in the work of Proust. It asserts to his unbelief the permanence of personality and the reality of art. It synthesises the moments of privilege and runs parallel to them.'[14] If music, theatre, and 'seeing' are all examples of the fundamental 'triumph' of art, Elizabeth Reegan becomes a kind of poet in her transformation of banal expression into a Beckettian poetry: '"Whatever people be waitin' for anyhow" repeated itself over and over, but it did not affect her, the words remained calm and complete as a landscape that she could gaze dispassionately on for ever.'[15] Malone reflects:

> Words and images run riot in my mind, pursuing, flying, clashing, merging, endlessly. But beyond this tumult there is a great calm, and a great indifference, never really to be troubled by anything again... I go back again to the light, to the fields I so longed to love, to the sky all astir with little white

clouds as white and light as snowflakes, to the life I could never manage, through my own fault perhaps, through pride, or pettiness, but I don't think so.[16]

While Malone in the circumstances of his dying days, and in the style of his 'play' is quite different from Elizabeth, there are many such similarities. But, in the end, there is a fundamental difference. The care she extends to the work of her homemaking is different from the kind of inventory or testament or story that Malone uses to structure his time. Her actions are a form of love:

> Things had to be taken in small doses to be enjoyed, she knew; but how that mean of measurement degraded and cheapened all passion for life and for truth, and though it had to go through human hell, a total love was the only way she had of approaching towards the frightful fulfilment of being resonant with her situation, and this was her whole terror and longing…her life with these others, their need and her own need, all their fear, drew her back into the activity of the day where they huddled in their frail and human love, together.[17]

Unlike Malone, she is moved by the light on the landscape, the concrete reality of things and other people, towards 'a prayer of praise': 'She could live her life through in its mystery, without any purpose, except to watch and bear witness…She was alive and being was her ridiculous glory as well as her pain.'[18] If Elizabeth is aware, as are Beckett's solitaries, of the pain of being and of non-being, her conclusion—to live her life as a 'mystery without any purpose'—is a 'way of seeing' that is surely close to McGahern's own vision. Close to the end, she accepts her existential state as the basis of her belief: 'She had come to life out of mystery and would return, it surrounded her life, it safely held it as by hands; she'd return into that which she could not know; she'd be consumed at last in whatever meaning her life had. Here she had none, none but to be, which in acceptance must be surely to love.'[19]

If Nothingness may be a condition of everyday life, and the Absurd a literary category with which McGahern was familiar, his sense of character goes back to a Flaubertian exactitude of psychological and social realism. It may even be appropriate to recall

McGahern's long absorption of Shakespeare and to imagine that, like Thomas Hardy, his solidity of characterization owes something to that tragic vision. Elizabeth Reegan struggles with her fate through the simple and ordinary routines of home, yet in her inner struggles she rises to great heights of grandeur; her inner monologues reflect a beauty of spirit, and the catharsis of her death has a nobility only granted to the heroes of tragedy. It has to be noted, however, that McGahern's medium is the novel and he borrows from Flaubert a deflating and ironic twist: a short chapter follows the death and burial of Elizabeth, as in *Madame Bovary*, following Emma's death, the effect of this in each case being to reaffirm the reality of life and time, continuing in the world of those who remain living, whatever the grandeur or banality of the protagonist's vision before death. The outer world remains, with a physical reality, and already it may be that McGahern is defining his vision against Beckett's; his remark that 'you never find place names in Beckett',[20] although only partially true, is a clear indication of McGahern's allegiance to a metaphysical reality which is preserved in a fiction grounded in realism.

There is no doubt that in trying to write a novel that would move beyond the autobiographical and generalize some truth about the human condition, McGahern's meditation on death in life is vitally connected to his most rooted feelings. In the way he chose to bring the reader close to his central character, to her pain and to her spiritual quest, he is guided by the desire to go beyond technique or philosophical ideas to an honesty of feeling. It is an extraordinary achievement for a young man in his mid-twenties to imagine himself inside the skin of a middle-aged woman dying of cancer, and the absoluteness of this identification runs through every sentence and scene. The intensity of the style—unrelenting in its desolation, beautiful in its wondrous precision—suggests that in going beyond himself McGahern was creating a necessary insight into the mystery of his own mother's final months and his own intimacy with her. His mother's sincere religious conviction is here transformed into a secular vision, drawing on his readings of Proust and Yeats most of all, and, perhaps, behind them a Wordsworthian belief in the power of imagination.

The echoes of Proust are everywhere, clear evidence of how much McGahern had taken him to heart. He was surely drawn to those parts of Proust's work where the death of his mother and of his grandmother are investigated and to Proust's underlying conviction regarding the 'spiritual knowledge which grief brings'. In *Time Regained*, Marcel returns to reflect on the death of his grandmother: 'It almost seems as though a writer's works, like the water in an artesian well, mount to a height which is in proportion to the depth to which suffering has penetrated his heart.'[21] McGahern is acting here on some of the deepest principles of his mentor's work, not in imitation of fictional form or style but on the level of imaginative identification with the essential vision of Proust's art. A confident belief in his own ability matches his need to create something permanent in defiance of the facts of change, decay, and death.

In *The Barracks*, McGahern wrote an utterly sincere fiction, an honest depiction of suffering in a style that elevated it to the level of the beautiful. The young author had learned much from Flaubert, but he did not follow him in the direction of a realism that gained its edge from detachment and irony. Elizabeth occupies her world, and it is seen with complete sympathy, even if there are comic and satirical touches to the depiction of Reegan, the guards in the barracks, and the larger society in which reality is merely the established routines and roles, conversation a game of clichés and performances. Like many novelists, McGahern is very conscious of the illusionary sense of reality that comforts people because it veils from them the horror of pain and desolation. But he, like Elizabeth Reegan, is intensely focused on the grotesque disjunction between private feeling and knowledge and this illusionary sense of the real. Behind his overall conception of this aspect of the novel lies 'The Death of Ivan Ilyich'. As in Tolstoy's novella, the end is inevitable and the fiction is shaped by this inevitability, but the writer's business is to bring the reader through the outer layers of conventional reality into an experience of time and suffering which feels redemptive. As the course of everyday life proceeds, the reader is engrossed not by plotting or outer drama but by the impassioned style which captures the movements of consciousness in a state of crisis.

One has a sense that McGahern's own experience of this disjunction was a truth of his spiritual life that he needed to master. The artificial life of the barracks routine, the pretence that work of some importance is being done, the 'patrols of the imagination', and the

structures of authority that elevate Reegan's sense of importance
were known to McGahern as an adolescent in Cootehall, and were
identified by the novelist as a first lesson in a Beckett-like sense of
'fabricated habits'. He also commented on the pretences he had to
maintain in his job as a teacher; he had to play the game in the
major emphasis on teaching the Irish language and a nationalistic
version of Irish history—the motivating forces for many of his colleagues—neither of which he really believed in. By and large, it is
clear that he felt the ruling class in the country, with de Valera as
its main icon, had invented comforting mythologies of national identity and culture; alienated from this chauvinism, he nevertheless kept
his thoughts to himself. More generally, the novel envelops Elizabeth
in an everyday world of routine actions, conversations, and gestures
that at times amount to a kind of theatre in which she is an interested spectator. Echoes of Shakespeare and Beckett add to a sense
of 'all the world's a stage, the men and women merely players'; at
times, this offers Elizabeth a kind of calm in detached observation,
at other times a craving for a way of being that will break through
illusion into a reality she can trust. In this she is surely the alter ego
of her creator.

McGahern is present in every detail of his book, and in a particular way in a central drama: the recalled relationship of Elizabeth
and Halliday in London, their love affair, their separation, and the
contrast between her life with him and with Reegan. These memories which recur at various points are not a strand of plotting designed to give interest to Elizabeth's characterization by depicting
her earlier life in London; it is an integral part of the working out
of her own vision, and, as in Proust, the vitality of recollection itself,
and its recurrence, are a proof of the significance of that earlier
time. 'In this café by the river images crowded every other source of
life out of her mind...She was in London, with Halliday, the enriched and indestructible days about her, "What the hell is all this
living and dying about anyway, Elizabeth? That's what I'd like to
know," removed to the fixity of death and memory and coming now
like a quality of laughter.'[22] Quite simply, her encounter with Halliday awakened a sense of her own individuality and the cultivation
of that sense as a primary reality was achieved in the light of their
love. His distinct individual presence, her discovery of literature as

a shared pleasure and a spiritual source, and the shock of his sudden death—he who had joked about suffering—all return to her, made more telling now as she sifts through her daily life for significance. She must do so in an affirmation of meaning that rejects Halliday's very articulated vision, although it had, at first, captivated her and remains part of her. His form of rational nihilism seemed to determine, or mirror, his early death, and now, even in the midst of absurdity, she wants to grasp whatever moments of wonder she can find in her present life.

Elizabeth's vivid recall of her years as a nurse in London during the war—Michael Halliday was a doctor—have an appropriateness to her present situation in that the Blitz made death a daily possibility that all must face. Their work in the hospital made pain and suffering their inescapable daily reality, a version of existentialism their practical credo. Yet perhaps there is another kind of appropriateness. They work at a hospital on Whitechapel Road in the East End, near Aldgate Street tube station, and there are many specific references to this neighbourhood:

> She didn't think she could go on only for the fact that often when she was alone her sense of the collapsing rubble of this actual day faded, and processions of dead days began to return haunting clear, it seemed in compensation. Her childhood and the wild smell of the earth in the evenings after spring rain and the midges swarming out of the trees; streets of London at all hours, groping for the Jewish names on the lintels—Frank, Levine, Lerner, Goldsberg, Botzmans—above the awnings in the little market off Commercial Road, and did the sun still glitter so on the red-stained glass over the little Yiddish Theatre, the left side of the road as you came from Aldgate.[23]

It was the part of the city McGahern himself had come to know in the summer of 1954, at a time when he was experiencing his own awakening to the consciousness of life without religious faith, to literature as an opening into another kind of reality, and to the responsibility of discovering meaning in one's life. As he remarked, 'consciousness begins with the sense of our future death'. What Elizabeth discovered with Halliday was what McGahern had discovered, and it might even be said that Halliday may represent the young man he became at that time. London was the setting of his first journey away from the enveloping unrealities of Irish life, and since his sisters, like Elizabeth, had qualified as nurses there, and he became a regular visitor to London, the place assumed a symbolic imaginative state for him. Most recently, even as the idea of the novel was forming, he had walked with Patrick Swift those very streets he had once known every day in the summer of 1954 and which he often recalled lovingly. London is, then, a counter world to the rural world of the barracks, and the inner drama of Elizabeth's re-engagement with the significance of Halliday and his vision of life may represent an inner debate that McGahern himself had experienced.

It is as if Elizabeth's vision may embody a more mature McGahern vision, the character of Halliday being a version of his younger self, although this character may reflect a more constant aspect of himself, for there are stories in *Nightlines*, written later than *The Barracks*, which might be said to 'revert' to the vision of Halliday. Inside the novel and in McGahern's early work generally there is a debate between nihilism and faith in life. The 'condemned man', the Outsider, is, in part, Elizabeth searching for her freedom, although it is also appropriate to see Halliday in this context for he is the example of the suicide. Camus's argument against suicide is not only in philosophical texts or fiction but also in his essays about the Mediterranean world of Algeria which McGahern really liked. If his characters share something of the philosophical concerns of Camus, these are set off against a more Catholic sense of mystery and the sacred, something that might be associated with McGahern's partiality for McLaverty's work, and, indeed, the ideas of Proust and Yeats which preserve that poetic sense of mystery. Indeed, in the way in which Halliday and Reegan are counterpointed in Elizabeth's consciousness, the novel may reflect McGahern's dialogue with Joyce's 'The Dead', which hinges on Gretta Conroy's recovery of the 'distant music' of her dead lover, Michael Furey.

While it is undoubtedly true that literary images and techniques from McGahern's extensive reading contributed to his way of envisioning and dramatizing the story of Elizabeth Reegan in the barracks, the world and style of the novel and the focused energy of its composition may owe something to the circumstances in which it was written between 1960 and 1962.

In early 1960, for instance, his sister Margaret was diagnosed with tuberculosis, and she spent six months in Blanchardstown sanatorium. She did recover, but during this year McGahern visited her regularly in the hospital, and he recalls that their father did not, a remark that suggests that the illness of Margaret stirred emotions embedded in him twenty years earlier when his father behaved enigmatically during his wife's illness and eventual death. McGahern's anger at his father's neglect of his daughter and at his final abandonment of his wife is obvious in *Memoir*, and, perhaps, a recognition that his father was emotionally incapable of dealing with death.

Another test in the summer of 1960 was the sudden death of Donncha Ó Céileachair, his friend in Belgrove School. McGahern had been in London, where he had met Tony Whelan, and he now wrote to him:

> It is so degrading to be back at school again. I was very close to the dead person. You see a door opening, and you imagine him where you have often seen him. He was younger looking than his years. You cannot see him again, that is the terrible thing, he no longer exists, as we ourselves will find the day when we can never see or be seen. And the fulsome obituaries make one embarrassed that are coming out in the Gaelic magazines. No wonder Yeats, an Irishman, said the sentimentalist deceives himself, the rhetorician his neighbours.[24]

Six months later, he refers to this death in a letter to McLaverty. He tells him that 'I first put your work in his way and it was a real sign of his love' that Ó Céileachair wanted to translate a work by McLaverty into Irish. 'It is a small thing, sentimental may be, but he had probably intended to tell you what I have said, and I feel easier that you should know.' Clearly McGahern has continued to be very moved by the death of his friend. 'He was a friend of mine', he tells McLaverty, 'and it is hardly for me to praise him; but it was generally believed that he was the only Gaelic writer of distinction or promise among those who were still young... Now that Ó Céileachair is dead the whole Gaelic business looks even more quixotic to

me than it was before.'[25] These brief words convey a depth of feeling
and identification, and a sense of a larger ending of hope and promise; it is surely significant that he should want to share such feelings
of desolation with the living writer whose friendship meant most to
him.

Is it too much to think that in facing the death of Ó Céileachair, in visiting his sister, as he will visit his mother's sister Maggie
in St Luke's cancer hospital not too long after this, and in visiting
John Jordan in Blanchardstown sanatorium in 1962, he is doing
something that his father was incapable of doing, and that his
novel is in a sense a visiting of the sick, a facing up to the reality
of suffering, fear, and death as facts of life? In writing of Elizabeth
Reegan, he was dramatizing and articulating a kind of maturity
his father never gained. This novel continues his preoccupation
with the sick-room, first noted in 'The Going' and repeated in *The
Leavetaking*, but after *The Barracks*, he will return in *The Pornographer*
to retell the story of a dying woman, this time reflecting the death
of his mother's sister, Maggie, and its protagonist will visit over
and over his dying aunt. These narratives are dramatized with
their differing thematic and formal preoccupations, but it may
also be that McGahern is drawn to these situations to reassure
himself that he is not the coward that his father was as his mother
lay dying. It is the ultimate test of his manhood, to accommodate
himself to the central fact of life. 'The idea of death took up permanent residence within me in the way that love sometimes does',
Proust wrote in *Time Regained*; 'the idea of death still kept me
company as faithfully as the idea of myself'.[26] Nuala O'Faolain,
who met McGahern just after he had finished writing *The Barracks*, commented: 'He had made himself into a true stoic. I don't
think I have ever met anyone who so fully accepted the way
things are. In the simplest way, he was always ready to die.'[27] She
is writing after his death, but in characterizing thus the man she
knew—'had made himself'—she is stating in brief the 'training' in
all the previous years, the reading of Beckett, Proust, and Tolstoy
on suffering, which cumulatively gave him a vision for his own
sense of death and redemption.

In late 1961, perhaps a year into the composition of the novel, he
outlined his plan to John Montague with the utmost clarity:

You felt the structure of the work fairly truly. There are the 3 opening chapters; a long IV in 4 distinct parts, the early time pattern gets completely broken up; and then 3 chapters in the manner of the first 3 leading away. I'm grateful for what you said about the first chapters. It'll all have to be revised again.

The husband and wife come vitally into Chapter IV and for the first time independently of the woman's vision. She dies in the second last chapter and the work ends in a triumph in violence for the less conscious vision, the social vision, before the children, who have only the function of a chorus, draw the blinds, as the novel began, on the mystery of another evening.

I think what you say of the need for structure true, but I think it must be *unique* or organic, growing out of the struggle with the material, and not a superimposed structure as in Joyce and Eliot.[28]

From the beginning, then, it appears that the 'organic' structure of the novel is an outgrowth of 'the woman's vision', counterpointed by the 'social vision', and the passage of time. The confidence in his artistic purpose and in his sense of a narrative that mirrors his individual vision is remarkable.

Just as he arrived at the final revisions, six months later, the author prepared another statement of his purpose and his method. It was a commentary submitted to the trustees of the Macaulay Prize at the time the novel was sent for their judgement, and, uniquely in McGahern's career, it provides precise insight into his aesthetic intentions in various episodes of a novel. He begins by stating that it is finished but not finally and so he is submitting only Chapter 5 (but, in fact, the trustees asked for more chapters later). His commentary opens with an admission that it was 'technically the most difficult chapter [because of its different treatment of time], but the chapter itself is no more important than any of the others'. This insistence on the equal significance of everything that happens is a philosophical statement of substantial importance for the aesthetic effect he has in mind:

As it is not a novel, but an attempt to break that form down into a religious poem, I can only hope to indicate some of the tones as it moves to its end. The vision is all that matters in it, and the style, for a banality in it can assume as much importance as the beautiful. What happens matters very little, the real things that happen are inevitable, and the others should be inevitable in the laws of the work itself.[29]

The claim that he has not written a conventional novel but 'a religious poem' is remarkable and has far-reaching implications for all the later work.

Describing his intentions in this chapter and in the novel as a whole, McGahern passes over the relationship of Elizabeth and Reegan. He highlights 'her growing vision of the morality involved in all relationships' and yet her sense is finally of 'the absurdity of trying to get some one to understand us', either her husband or the priest in Confession. Guard Mullins wishes to share a private feeling with her, but she 'doesn't accept this invitation, she presents him with what he wants to see, deliberately dishonest because of no belief in the possibility of communication'. That gap of incomprehension is at the heart of works that inspired McGahern in these years: from Tolstoy's 'The Death of Ivan Ilyich' and Melville's 'Bartleby the Scrivener' to Kafka's 'Metamorphosis', Pirandello's plays, and Beckett's solitaries, in particular Malone.

Elizabeth is alone with her pain and the realization that she is dying:

> She experiences the beauty of the things about her with increasing violence...In the end all things are lost in contemplation...She is finally driven to rest on the idea of God, not any personal or particular God, but the Explanation of the apparent futility and unreason of their lives. There would be no search in heaven. We would grow into our Meaning as we grew into love. There was that or nothing and she couldn't lose.

Rather than find any meaning in the lives of those around her, the policemen and their wives, the children, her husband, the priest, or doctor, she finds some solace in discovering how her feelings and thoughts follow the round of the year, although 'Nature tells nothing: it is as silent in the work as God is.' Her vision is indeed a bleak one as far as any trust or belief in other humans is concerned, yet McGahern insists otherwise for she maintains 'her whole passion for life and for truth' and 'though, or because, it had to go through appalling suffering total love was the only means we had of approaching the frightful fulfilment of being resonant with our situation'. The fundamental principle seems to be hinted at here, that Meaning and 'total love' come unawares, not rationally, and that they grow out of suffering. The wilful effort of Reegan to conquer his nemesis, Superintendent Quirke, is contrasted with Elizabeth's visionary morality: 'there is a bare hint that he didn't find all he expected in the satisfaction of years of hatred'. Elizabeth is closer in spirit to the children than to her husband, although they are not her biological children; they are described as 'a chorus in the work', and 'it is left to them to close it in the same way as it opened, and to affirm the final sense of mystery'.

Such an unintentional discovery and reaffirmation of the capacity for love and meaning and the insistence on final mystery recalls the Proustian discovery of the essential self through involuntary memory, and, although McGahern does not stress in this statement the central place of memory in Elizabeth's life, the novel demonstrates that this is so. It is in these terms that the novel becomes a 'religious poem'; a few months earlier, he wrote to McLaverty: 'all art approaches prayers'. Her need *in extremis* mirrors his own passionate need for a vision of life. It is a young man's book, her alienation and compromises to a degree a young man's view of a lost and absurd life, and yet his need leads him to have Elizabeth go back over her life and reject the nihilism of Halliday. He wanted the book to be 'a prayer of praise', and this it accomplishes not so much in its philosophical statements but in the degree of sympathy it brings to the depiction of Elizabeth and her world. The reader is brought so close to her as she follows her saintly spiritual quest that the fiction itself becomes an image of its creator's own belief in life even in the most extreme circumstances of disbelief. It is not only the *via* of a character in fiction that is dramatized here but the *via* of its author.

Epilogue

The 'long secret life of reading and writing', the 'years of training in the secret Dublin years', ended for McGahern in 1962 with the completion of *The Barracks*, the publication of extracts from it, and the award of an admired literary prize that was reported in the national press. But to McLaverty he wrote that the attention the work was receiving left him unmoved and that 'all success and failure are *private*'; he insisted that 'the inscrutable face of the work' was the primary reality for him and his effort to find in it an appropriate response to 'all the human suffering about us'.[1] He had told McLaverty and Whelan earlier of his dissatisfaction with his work as a teacher, and he now wrote to John Montague that 'I hope to leave this school and go abroad when I've this work finished.' Montague had left Dublin and was now living in Paris, where McGahern visited him in the summer, after spending a few weeks in London. At that time he wrote to McLaverty 'I feel broken after it, that is all', and later 'I came to almost the end of my world after finishing the book.' The poised statement of his artistic achievement in the novel, which he wrote in May for the Macaulay Prize trustees, belies the sense of restlessness and exhaustion, finality, in his private struggle with himself. He continued to revise and polish the novel until he submitted it to Charles Monteith in mid-June, but already the shape of the future was beginning to appear.

At this time when he had to begin to consider what kind of public role or persona as artist he wished to convey, a special kind of pressure on his private work as artist emerged which within a few years will come to have a very public impact on his life. In all his public retrospective comments on censorship in Ireland, he shrugged it off as having little effect on his real work as a writer. Yet the private circumstances were different. In a letter to John Montague regarding the extract from *The Barracks* that would be included in *The Dolmen*

Miscellany, he raised an issue that was clearly on his mind: 'The *fucking* can hardly cause trouble, it has no sexual significance, it only lights the breakdown of civility.'[2] Montague did not object, but when the completed manuscript reached Monteith, he did. There followed consultations with legal and literary advisors which continued until September. In the end, the objectionable word was removed from Reegan's dialogue although McGahern refused to remove it from Halliday's dialogue because in this case he believed that to do so would harm the work, nor would he accept a suggested compromise of 'f----'.[3] Towards the end of the year, when proofs arrived, he was shocked to discover that that this was the form given to the word, and Monteith, blaming a prurient printer for this, agreed to allow the complete spelling.

With this first novel then, McGahern was already aware that the thrust of his work was implicitly at odds with the 'censorship mentality', which he now discovered prevailed even in publishing circles in London. Two years after the celebrated prosecution and trial of Penguin Books for publishing *Lady Chatterley's Lover*, a case in which Penguin was found by a jury to be not guilty, there was still anxiety at Faber and Faber regarding the f-word. Of course, there was also the celebrated case of Edna O'Brien, whose first novel, *The Country Girls*, was banned in Ireland in 1960 and her second, *The Lonely Girl*, in 1962, although she did not use the f-word in either. In general, the Irish Censorship Board appeared to make the point that nothing had changed and that the younger generation of writers was not to imagine they were free to write as they wished. McGahern's claim later that the banning of *The Dark* in 1965 came as a complete surprise draws attention away from what he knew about a tendency in his own work from the summer of 1962. His resistance and rebellion would become an explicit part of his aesthetic for it is surely intentional that F-U-C-K appears on the first page of the next novel. McGahern knew, and Monteith knew, that he was issuing a direct challenge, an aesthetic and moral challenge that would almost certainly bring down the house for him. Predictably, it did, in 1965 when *The Dark* was banned, and some months later he was fired from his teaching position amidst much public debate of his case. By then, he was already in exile from Ireland, and he would remain in this condition for a decade.

In the months after finishing the novel, McGahern turned his attention to the writing of short stories, and within a year wrote and had published the first stories of a long sequence that eventually won him as much esteem as his career as a novelist. These stories of childhood may have been drafted earlier, perhaps even as early as 1959, when, after hearing Michael McLaverty and other writers discuss stories of childhood at a public event in University College Dublin, he had initiated the correspondence with McLaverty, much of which includes references to stories they have been reading. Their scope is wide—Russian, American, French, Irish—and while the established Irish writers of stories appeared to claim a special gift and a special tradition of Irish narrative, McGahern rejected this idea of a tradition and had a low opinion of their work. Yet his contacts with Mary Lavin and Elizabeth Cullinan, whose work was appearing regularly in the *New Yorker*, may have nourished his ambition to try the short genre at this stage.

In August 1962, McGahern sent 'Coming into his Kingdom' to Mary Lavin's editor at the *New Yorker*. It was rejected in September 1962, but a year later the story was included in the *Kilkenny Magazine* and in an anthology, *Voices*, published in London by Michael Joseph, Mary Lavin's publisher for many years. In December, the *New Yorker* wrote to tell him they had accepted a second story, 'Strandhill, the Sea', but a story close to his heart, 'The Going', was rejected in March 1963. He made one other try with the *New Yorker*, sending on 'Something for Himself' in September 1963, but this story of Christmas, later to be known as 'Christmas', was rejected. By then, 'Strandhill, the Sea' had appeared, renamed 'Summer in Strandhill', and it seems that the heavy-handed editorial pencil on that story had been too much for McGahern. He did not send new stories to the magazine for many years, and, in fact, he appears to have put aside all work on stories for a few years as the writing of *The Dark* came to occupy his complete attention.

A few years later, however, he commented to Brian Friel: 'The N.Y. took one story, which they buggered about with no end... I think they think my work is too rough or something.'[4] It amounted to another kind of censorship. These experiences in 1962–3 made him self-conscious about the 'rough' aspects of his work, and *The Dark*, certain stories in *Nightlines*, and *The Pornographer* are all marked by an assertion of his right to be as 'rough' as he finds it necessary to be for the truth of his evolving vision. He became as fastidious in capturing the roughness of life as the lyrical, the transcendent, or the sublime, and this arose from his need for freedom of thought and imagination and a moral defiance of the 'censorship mentality'.

In February–March 1963, the reviews of *The Barracks* were unanimously laudatory in both Dublin and London newspapers.[5] The anonymous reviewer in the *Times Literary Supplement* praised its 'formal, graceful prose that rises effortlessly to the moving occasion', and David Lodge remarked on its 'scrupulous yet enhancing accuracy', appearing to acknowledge a debt to the early work of Joyce and countering the impression of 'scrupulous meanness'. In March it was top of the list of 'What Dublin is Reading'. Bruce Arnold spoke for many in his eloquent review in the *Irish Times*: 'It is, finally, for this simplicity of word and thought, this spare singleness of purpose in the writing, the poetic accuracy of 'the year *shifting*' and 'the first *waste* of the orchards' that I shall go back and read this book again. It is deservedly a prize-winner.'[6] Arnold's praise for the poetry of the prose, the 'phrase, image, tone and colour', the 'resilience and supple strength' of the writing must have pleased the young novelist. One review that certainly pleased him came from an unexpected quarter, the *Irish Independent*; its columnist John D. Sheridan described it as 'classical tragedy', and McGahern noted this in *Memoir* many decades later.

Clearly, such critical acclaim—so uniformly solid, in fact, that the novel remained in the eyes of some readers his finest achievement—was focused as he would wish on the aesthetic qualities of his vision. Bruce Arnold's remark that the novel includes 'an endless search for the meaning that lies behind the action, when the action itself should and must be meaning enough' pinpoints how McGahern embodied in a work of poetic realism a profound questioning of meaning itself. It is the depth of that questioning, without resolution except in the style of the prose, Elizabeth's 'way of seeing', that gives the book its moral stature and makes it a classic novel. He had vindicated his decision to abandon 'The End or the Beginning of Love' and had realized the kind of achievement he had spoken of to Patrick Swift in rejecting 'the autobiographical stunt'.

From his discovery of modern literature as a means of examining one's own life in the perspective of age-old human concerns, John McGahern had over a decade made himself into an artist. The poetic depth of his style mirrored his explorations of selfhood in Irish circumstances, and long before his mastery was recognized worldwide in novels such as *Amongst Women* and *That They May Face the Rising Sun*, he had written the classic novel out of which all his later achievement would grow.

Notes

Abbreviations used in notes

Published work by John McGahern:

B   *The Barracks* (London: Faber and Faber, 1963)
D   *The Dark* (London: Faber and Faber, 1965)
L   *The Leavetaking* (London: Faber and Faber, 1974; 1984) rev. edn.
P   *The Pornographer* (London: Faber and Faber, 1979)
AW   *Amongst Women* (London: Faber and Faber, 1990)
PD   *The Power of Darkness* (London: Faber and Faber, 1991)
CS   *The Collected Stories* (London: Faber and Faber 1992)
M   *Memoir* (London: Faber and Faber, 2006) *All Will be Well*
        (New York: Knepf, 2006)
CE   *Creatures of the Earth: New and Selected Stories* (London: Faber
        and Faber, 2006)
LW   *Love of the World: Essays* (London: Faber and Faber, 2009)

For *McL* see Ch.1 n.16; For *P71* see Ch.2 n.24.

Preface

1. Interview with Rosa Gonzalez, 1994, in J. Hurtley, Rosa Gonzalez, Ines Praga, and Esther Aliaga (eds.), *Ireland in Writing: Interviews with Writers and Academics* (Amsterdam and Atlanta: Rodopi, 1998), 42. While this idea has been expressed by various writers, one in particular may have been McGahern's source: 'I am persuaded that our intellects at twenty contain all the truths we shall ever find, but as yet we do not know truths that belong to us from opinions caught up in casual irritation or momentary fantasy. As life goes on we discover that certain thoughts sustain us in defeat, or give us victory, whether over ourselves or others, and it is these thoughts, tested by passion, that we call convictions.' William H. O'Donnell and Douglas N. Archibald (eds.), *The Collected Works of W. B. Yeats: Autobiographies* (New York: Scribner, 1999), 163.
2. LW 7. 'The Image [1991]' is a slightly revised version of 'The Image: Prologue to a Reading at the Rockefeller University [1968]'; this reading in New York took place in February 1966.
3. Published in New York as *By the Lake* (Knopf, 2002).
4. LW 345. 'Getting Flaubert's Facts Straight'.
5. Seamus Heaney, 'Shedding the Skin of Youth', *Sunday Independent*, 26 January 1975: 9.
6. LW 9. 'Playing with Words'.

1. Pleasure and Knowledge

1. LW 107–8. 'Schooldays: A Time of Grace'.
2. D 124.
3. Ibid., 188.
4. LW 88–9. 'The Solitary Reader'.
5. Ibid., 90.
6. Named Seán Augustine McGahern, he continued all his life to be known to family members as Seán, but at the end of the 1950s he began to use the first name John with new friends. For instance, his first letter to the novelist Michael McLaverty, dated January 1959, is signed John, whereas letters to Tony Whelan, whom he had known since 1953, continue past this time to be signed Seán. All his published work appears under the name John.
7. 'Education and the Arts: The Educational Autobiographies of Contemporary Irish Poets, Novelists, Dramatists, Musicians, Painters and Sculptors: A Research Report' (School of Education, Trinity College Dublin, 1987), XIII, 138. Quotations in this and the following paragraph are taken from this report, which includes a profile based on an interview.
8. M 169.
9. L 37.
10. Ibid., 38.
11. D 146.
12. Ibid., 140.
13. Ibid., 128.
14. I first suggested the importance of Shakespeare to McGahern in *Outstaring Nature's Eye* and briefly considered the relevance of the idea of the tragic hero in 'The Solitary Hero', a lecture at the John McGahern International Seminar in 2009, later published in *The John McGahern Yearbook*, 3. Stanley van der Ziel has also identified allusions to Shakespeare in his PhD dissertation, 'Medusa's Mirror: Art, Style, Vision and Tradition in the Fiction of John McGahern' (UCD, 2008).
15. L 38.
16. John Killen (ed.), *Dear Mr. McLaverty: The Literary Correspondence of John McGahern and Michael McLaverty 1959–1980* (Belfast: Linen Hall Library, 2006), 42. Abbreviated in following notes to *McL*.
17. M 199–201.
18. Ibid., 203.
19. L 77.
20. CE viii.
21. LW 90. 'The Solitary Reader'.
22. 'A Conversation with John McGahern', *Canadian Journal of Irish Studies* 17(1) (July 1991): 13.
23. 'The Solitary Reader', *CJIS*, 17(1) (July 1991): 21. This passage differs from the text of the essay included in LW.

2. The Vocation

1. My thanks to Mary Shine Thompson of St Patrick's College of Education for showing me the registration records. The details of McGahern's registration at University College, Galway (now NUI Galway) and his withdrawal are taken from Seamus O'Grady, 'John McGahern and the University', in *John McGahern at NUI (Galway*: 2007), 13–14.
2. M 208.
3. Ibid., 205.
4. LW 207. '*Dubliners*'.
5. LW 133. 'The Church and its Spire'.
6. Ibid.,143.
7. 'Education and the Arts', 138.
8. Ibid., 139.
9. Reminiscences by McGahern's classmate Bernie O'Sullivan were provided by him to Eoghan Ó Suilleabháin of St Patrick's Department of Education, and I am grateful to Professor Ó Suilleabháin for allowing me to have a copy.
10. LW 115.
11. *McL*, 18.
12. M 213.
13. Ibid., 242.
14. Ibid., 261.
15. 'John McGahern', in Clíodhna Ní Anluain (ed.), *Reading the Future: Irish Writers in Conversation with Mike Murphy* (Dublin: RTE, 2000), 146.
16. Arminta Wallace, 'Out of the Dark: An Interview with John McGahern', *Irish Times*, 28 April 1990, Weekend 5.
17. M 213.
18. AW 35.
19. Ibid., 143.
20. M 210.
21. Tony Whelan, 'Working at the Mill', *John McGahern Yearbook*, 2, 28. See also Tony Whelan, *The Last Chapter: A Memoir* (Leicester: Matador, 2010).
22. M 213.
23. B 87.
24. P71/563. The John McGahern Papers, James Hardiman Library Archives, National University of Ireland Galway. All further references to material in the archives will be identified by the short form, P71/…, according to the Catalogue of the Papers prepared by Fergus Fahey.
25. M 217.
26. Ibid., 216.
27. Letter to C. M. Newman, 1 June 1963, *New Yorker* Records, Manuscripts and Archives Division, New York Public Library.
28. See Tom French, 'The Hummingbird of Athboy', *John McGahern Yearbook*, 3, 26–35. I am indebted to Tom French for an email cor-

respondence and for further research which in the end failed to clarify how long McGahern actually spent teaching in Athboy before moving to Drogheda. In McGahern's own accounts, there is conflicting evidence: 'My Education' elides Athboy completely, stating that he spent a year in Drogheda (LW 113), and this is repeated in 'The Church and its Spire' (LW 142); *Memoir* reports that 'I soon moved from there to Drogheda' (M 218); Tony Whelan reports visiting him in Drogheda; but the evidence collected by Tom French in Athboy suggests that he remained there for much of the year 1955–6.

29. M 224.
30. PD vii.
31. M 242.
32. Ibid., 222.
33. LW 116. '*Ní bheidh sibh ar ais*: St Patrick's College Drumcondra'.
34. M 240.
35. Ibid.
36. *The Leavetaking* (London: Faber and Faber, 1974), 92. This passage was deleted from the rev. edn.
37. M 241.
38. 'Rhythm, Images, and the Fiction of John McGahern: An Interview', *An Gael* 3(2) (Winter 1986): 13.
39. LW 303. 'A Bank of Non-Sequiturs'.

3. 'The years of training in the secret Dublin years'

1. Interview with John McGahern, 17 November 1993, in *La Licorne* 32 (Special issue on John McGahern) (1995): 26.
2. Details on the Swift family taken from Veronica O'Mara, 'Patrick Swift: A Short Life' in Veronica O'Mara (ed.), *PS...of course: Patrick Swift 1927–1983* (Oysterhaven, Co. Cork: Gandon Books, 1993).
3. 'Q&A with John McGahern', *Irish Literary Supplement* 3(1) (Spring 1984): 40.
4. LW 70. 'The Bird Swift'.
5. John Jordan, 'Joyce without Fears' in John Ryan and Myles na Gopaleen (eds.), *A Bash in the Tunnel: Joyce by the Irish* (London: Clifton Books, 1970), 141.
6. 'Education and the Arts', 139.
7. LW 92. 'The Solitary Reader'.
8. Antoinette Quinn, *Patrick Kavanagh: A Biography* (Dublin: Gill and Macmillan, 2003), 350–3.
9. LW 330–1. 'Journey Along the Canal Bank'.
10. Antoinette Quinn (ed.), *Collected Poems of Patrick Kavanagh* (London: Allen Lane, 2004), 181.
11. Ibid., 208.
12. Ibid., 129.

13. Ibid., 217.
14. Anthony Cronin, 'Innocence and Experience: The Poetry of Patrick Kavanagh', *Nimbus* 3(4) (Winter 1956): 20–3.
15. Apart from the classic memoirs of this period in Dublin literary life by Anthony Cronin, *Dead as Doornails*, and John Ryan, *Remembering Where We Stood*, Brian Fallon's *An Age of Innocence, Irish Culture 1930–1960* (Dublin: Gill and Macmillan, 1998), provides a useful historical overview of such figures and their intellectual contexts.
16. P71/1177.
17. Alan Simpson, *Beckett and Behan and a Theatre in Dublin* (London: Routledge and Kegan Paul, 1962).
18. *La Licorne*: 66, 76–7.
19. Peter Lennon, *Foreign Correspondent: Paris in the Sixties* (London: Picador, 1994).
20. LW 98. 'Censorship'. Lines quoted by McGahern are from 'If Ever You Go to Dublin Town', Patrick Kavanagh, *Collected Poems*, 193.
21. Interview with Patrick Godon, *The Scrivener: A Literary Magazine* (Summer 1984): 25.
22. LW 261–2.

4. 'Writing all the time'

1. *John McGahern Yearbook*, 2, 31. Letter to Tony Whelan, 16 July 1958, reproduced on 32–3.
2. P 24.
3. *The Collected Poems of W. B. Yeats* (London: Macmillan, 1950), 156.
4. This key sentence is taken from Proust's Preface to his translation of Ruskin's *Sesame and Lilies*, later revised as an essay, 'Days of Reading'. It is likely that McGahern read it in *Pleasures and Days and Other Writings by Marcel Proust*, ed. F. W. Dupee (New York: Doubleday Anchor, 1957), 215; in this collection, the essay is entitled 'Ruskin and Others', but in a more recent translation by John Sturrock in *Against Sainte-Beuve and Other Essays* (London: Penguin, 1988), the essay is entitled 'Days of Reading'.
5. Letter to C. M. Newman, 16 February 1963. *New Yorker* Records, New York Public Library.
6. All quotations in this discussion of the 'London' fiction are taken from P71/3.
7. D 142.
8. *John McGahern Yearbook*, 2, 32.

5. 'Art is solitary man'

1. LW 91–2. 'The Solitary Reader'.
2. M 243.
3. LW 94. 'The Solitary Reader'.

4. *Pleasures and Days*, 215–16.

5. This sentence is taken from a passage in Yeats's diary of 1909, first published in *Estrangement*, 1926: 'All civilisation is held together by the suggestions of an invisible hypnotist—by artificially created illusions. The knowledge of reality is always in some measure a secret knowledge. It is a kind of death.' *Autobiographies*, 356.

6. LW 92. 'The Solitary Reader'.

7. L 38.

8. *Mythologies* (London: Macmillan, 1959), 332.

9. *Autobiographies*, 80–1. First included in *Reveries over Childhood and Youth* (1916).

10. My earlier study *Outstaring Nature's Eye: The Fiction of John McGahern* (Washington, DC: Catholic University of America Press, and Dublin: Lilliput Press, 1993), identifies many points in McGahern's fiction where Yeats's work is recalled. See also Frank Shovlin, 'The ghost of W. B. Yeats', *John McGahern Yearbook*, 2, 42–51.

11. LW 246. 'The Letters of John Butler Yeats'. Same citation for quotations in following paragraph.

12. John Butler Yeats, *Letters to his son W. B. Yeats and Others 1869–1922*, ed. Joseph Hone; abridged and with an Introduction by John McGahern (London: Faber and Faber, 1999), 67–8. The original Hone edition, most likely the one known to McGahern, was published in 1944.

13. Ibid., 137.

14. This sentence and, indeed, McGahern's reference to the 'moral activity' of mature reading, which he associated with Yeats, are taken from this passage in Yeats's diary of 1909, first published in *The Death of Synge* (1928): 'The element which in men of action corresponds to style in literature is the moral element. Books live almost entirely because of their style, and the men of action who inspire movements after they are dead are those whose hold upon impersonal emotion and law lifts them out of immediate circumstances...Men are dominated by self-conquest; thought that is a little obvious or platitudinous if merely written, becomes persuasive, immortal even, if held to amid the hurry of events. The self-conquest of the writer who is not a man of action is style.' *Autobiographies*, 381.

15. *La Licorne*, 84.

16. Ibid., 26.

17. Lionel Gallagher, 'Seán and I: A Tale of Two Barracks', *Leitrim Guardian, 2010*, 163.

18. LW 185. 'Mr Joyce and Mr Yeats'.

19. Letter to John Montague, undated, mid-December 1961, John Montague fonds, Archives and Special Collections, University of Victoria, British Columbia.

20. LW 201. '*Dubliners*'.

21. Ibid., 205.

22. Ibid., 202.
23. Ibid., 204.
24. Ibid., 206.
25. Stanislaus Joyce, *My Brother's Keeper: James Joyce's Early Years* (New York: Viking, 1958), 164.
26. Ibid., 180.
27. Ibid., 185.
28. *Pleasures and Days*, 182.
29. Ibid., 198.
30. Ibid., 201.
31. Ibid., 203.
32. Ibid., 215–16.
33. 'A Conversation with John McGahern', 17.
34. Ibid.
35. Sturrock, *Against Sainte-Beuve*, 318.
36. Ibid., 319.
37. *Pleasures and Days*, 206.
38. See my essays 'The Lost Image: Some Notes on McGahern and Proust', *Canadian Journal of Irish Studies* 17(1) (July 1991): 57–68, and on his last work, 'The 'sacred weather' of County Leitrim: John McGahern's *Memoir*', *Irish Review* 36–7 (Winter 2007): 120–8.
39. 'A Conversation with John McGahern', 17.
40. Samuel Beckett, *Proust* (1931, repr. New York: Grove Press, n.d.), 49, 56, 60, 66, 67. It might be noted that this last sentence is repeated word for word by McGahern in describing Joyce's style in '*Dubliners*', and some of the others are closely echoed in that essay of 1990.
41. See Stanley van der Ziel, 'John McGahern: *Nightlines*' in Cheryl Alexander Malcolm and David Malcolm (eds.), *A Companion to the British and Irish Short Story* (Malden, Mass., and Oxford: Wiley-Blackwell, 2008), 488–97.
42. Samuel Beckett, *Malone Dies* (1958, repr. Harmondsworth: Penguin, 1962), 14.
43. CE 3.
44. LW 264. 'What Is My Language?'

6. The Character of the Local Artist

1. P71/1310. Text of a talk at the launch of the Patrick Kavanagh, *Collected Poems*, 13 October 2004.
2. LW 331. 'Journey along the Canal Bank'.
3. LW 68. 'The Bird Swift'.
4. The poet depicted in the story 'Bank Holiday' is unmistakably Kavanagh, and McGahern told the anecdote regarding the protagonist's refusal to cooperate with the poet elsewhere, so that in this instance it may be assumed that these words reflect McGahern's own viewpoint.
5. LW 331. 'Journey along the Canal Bank'.

6. Ibid., 333.

7. M 243.

8. LW 75. 'A Poet Who Worked in Prose: Memories of Michael McLaverty'. McGahern misremembered that the event was a meeting of the L&H, probably because it was held in the Physics Theatre in Earlsfort Terrace. McLaverty was a panel member, along with Benedict Kiely, James Plunkett, and John Jordan, who all responded to the auditor's paper entitled '"The Questioning Iris"—The Child in the Modern Irish Short Story'. The date was 28 February 1958.

9. LW 76.

10. *McL*, 18. Letter 22 August 1959.

11. Ibid., 16. Letter 13 January 1959.

12. Ibid., 21. Letter 9 March 1960.

13. Ibid., 20.

14. Sophia Hillan King (ed.), *In Quiet Places: The Uncollected Stories, Letters and Critical Prose of Michael McLaverty* (Dublin: Poolbeg Press, 1989), 169. Journal entries 25 March 1953 and 7 September 1953.

15. Seamus Heaney, Introduction, Michael McLaverty, *Collected Short Stories* (Dublin: Poolbeg, 1978), 7–9. All quotations in this paragraph from this.

16. LW 75–6. 'A Poet Who Worked in Prose'.

17. Daniel Corkery, *The Threshold of Quiet* (Dublin: Phoenix Publishing, 1917), 192.

18. Ibid., 310.

19. LW 198. '*Brian Westby*'. See Reid, *W. B. Yeats: A Critical Study* (London: Secker, 1915), 218.

20. LW 198–9.

21. Ibid., 194.

22. Ibid., 199.

23. M 222.

24. Interview with James Whyte, March 1992, included as an appendix in James Whyte, *History, Myth and Ritual in the Fiction of John McGahern: Strategies for Transcendence* (Lampeter: Edwin Mellen Press, 2002), 230.

25. Ibid., 231.

26. Ibid.

27. Note, for instance, 'Some Notes on Caravaggio', *Nimbus* 3(4) (Winter 1956): 33–7: 'His genius operates in that world of antithesis where the conflict between ideal and reality rages, and the moral victory, i.e., the ultimate affirmation of the goodness of life is always so tenuously won that we feel the dread of chaos intensely–even when he is completely successful...But since he is wholly innocent beneath the apparent evidence of corruption he ends by moving us in a profound and religious way...It might further define their existence to say that Rembrandt's vision could only have been produced from a Protestant point of departure, whereas Caravaggio is conspicuously Catholic and Latin in temperament.' Swift's examination of a painting demonstrates how 'it is

religious in so far as it presents a deeply honest and passionate view of man' and in its 'profound declaration of the sacred importance of the innate character of each particular Thing to the painter'.

28. Donat O'Donnell (C. C. O'Brien), *Maria Cross: Imaginative Patterns in a Group of Modern Catholic Writers* (London: Chatto and Windus, 1954). Note also, for instance, Kate O'Brien, *Teresa of Avila* (New York: Sheed and Ward, 1951), and much of her fiction of the 1940s and 1950s, and travel writing set in Spain; and Seán O'Faolain, *Newman's Way: The Odyssey of John Henry Newman* (London: Longmans, Green, 1952), and his travel writings on Italy.

29. LW 5. 'The Image: Prologue to a Reading at Rockefeller University [1968]'.

30. M 222.

31. On Dodds, see LW 151, 'God and Me', and LW 323, 'From "Critic's Choice"'.

32. M 272.

33. Interview with James Whyte, 230.

7. 'The End or the Beginning of Love'

1. All quotations from the unpublished story 'The Going' are taken from P71/74.

2. P71/70.

3. All quotations from the unpublished novel 'The End or the Beginning of Love' are taken from P71/9.

4. M 272.

5. L 86–7.

6. D 48.

7. Patrick Kavanagh, *Collected Poems*, 173.

8. 'Prelude', ibid., 208.

8. 'The abiding life'

1. *McL*, 18. Letter 22 August 1959.

2. LW 207. '*Dubliners*'.

3. *McL*, 19. Letter 15 February 1960.

4. Letter to Michael McLaverty, undated [late 1961?], McLaverty papers, Linen Hall Library; John Killen, the Head Librarian, kindly agreed to search the papers for unpublished letters and provided me with a copy.

5. *McL*, 20–1. Letter 9 March 1960.

6. Leo Tolstoy, *War and Peace*, vol. II, trans. Rosemary Edmonds (Harmondsworth: Penguin, 1957), 1146.

7. Ibid., 1198.

8. Ibid., 1160.

9. Ibid., 1167.

10. Leo Tolstoy, *Childhood, Boyhood, Youth*, trans. Rosemary Edmonds (Harmondsworth: Penguin, 1964), 18. First translation into English, 1930.

11. *McL*, 18: 'I thought—especially in "My Husband and I"—I saw the seeds of Proust's great novel.'

12. *Childhood*, 91.

13. Ibid., 100.

14. Ibid., 103.

15. PD vii. I would like to acknowledge here a review by Ninian Mellamphy of *Outstaring Nature's Eye* in which he drew attention to my neglect of Tolstoy in that work.

16. Patrick Swift, 'Official Art and the Modern Painter', *X: A Quarterly Review of Literature and the Arts*, I(1) (1959), repr. David Wright (ed.), *An Anthology from 'X'* (Oxford: Oxford University Press, 1988), 17.

17. Ibid., 17.

18. LW 69. 'The Bird Swift'.

19. Ibid., 71.

20. Ibid., 74.

21. Ibid.

22. Ibid., 73.

23. All quotations in these paragraphs from an unpublished letter to Patrick Swift, 5 September 1960; The *X* Mss, Manuscript Collections, Lilly Library, University of Indiana.

24. *McL*, 19. Letter 15 February 1960.

25. *McL*, 20. Letter 9 March 1960.

26. Tom Kilroy, Foreword to Mary Lavin, *In a Café: Selected Stories* (Dublin: Town House and Country House, 1995). See also Leah Levinson, *The Four Seasons of Mary Lavin* (Dublin: Marino, 1998), 124–6.

27. Michael McLaverty, letter to Horace Reynolds, 16 January 1949, *In Quiet Places*, 129.

28. See *The Four Seasons of Mary Lavin*, 126–31.

29. Elizabeth Cullinan, letter to author, 25 August 2006.

30. Nuala O'Faolain, *Are You Somebody? The Accidental Memoir of a Dublin Woman* (Dublin: New Island Books, 1996; repr. New York: Henry Holt, 1998), 74. Letters quoted from are not dated.

31. Nuala O'Faolain, obituary column, *Sunday Tribune*, 2 April 2006, Tribune Review, 4.

32. The executors of the McGahern estate, Neil Belton, Senior Editor, and Robert Brown, archivist, Faber and Faber, kindly facilitated my reading of McGahern's correspondence with his editors at Faber and Faber; some details in this and the following paragraph are taken from the Faber and Faber files.

33. LW 99–100. 'Why the Booker Is Such a Hard Bet'.

34. *McL*, 33. This undated letter to Michael McLaverty should be assigned to January 1963, rather than January 1964, since McLaverty's letter to

McGahern dated 25 November 1962 mentions sending on the autobiography of Edwin Muir.

35. Ibid., 32. Letter 7 December 1963; this appears to have been misdated by McGahern; internal evidence indicates that it was written in 1962.
36. Ibid., 33. Undated letter [January 1963?].

9. Writing *The Barracks*

1. B 50.
2. Ibid., 57.
3. Ibid.
4. Ibid., 51.
5. Ibid., 73.
6. Ibid., 176–7.
7. *La Licorne*, 81.
8. See *Outstaring Nature's Eye*, Ch. 1, 'The Barracks: Suffering, Memory, and Vision', 33–60, for a more complete examination of the art of the novel and the evolution of Elizabeth's vision.
9. *La Licorne*, 77.
10. B 174.
11. Ibid., 134–5.
12. Ibid., 188.
13. Ibid., 135–6.
14. *Proust*, 71.
15. B 185–6.
16. *Malone Dies*, 30.
17. B 152.
18. Ibid., 94,
19. Ibid., 211.
20. 'A Conversation with John McGahern', 15.
21. Marcel Proust, *Time Regained*, trans. Andreas Mayor and Terence Kilmartin (London: Vintage, 1996), 270.
22. B 86.
23. Ibid., 186.
24. Letter to Tony Whelan undated [September 1960?]. My thanks to Tony Whelan for providing me with a copy of this letter.
25. *McL*, 24. Letter 21 January 1962; this letter was actually written in 1961. McGahern's heartfelt reaction to his friend's death may also be gauged by the fact that he began to write something about him; see P71/1319.
26. *Time Regained*, 445.
27. Nuala O'Faolain, obituary column, 4.
28. Letter to John Montague, undated, mid-December 1961.
29. All quotations in these paragraphs from P71/28.

Epilogue

1. *McL*, 25–6. Letters July 1962 and 20 September 1962.
2. Letter to John Montague, undated [mid-December 1961].
3. This outline of the novelist's first brush with censorship over the summer and autumn of 1962 is based on the correspondence files in the archives of Faber and Faber.
4. Letter to Brian Friel, undated [early 1968?], MS 37, 259, Brian Friel Papers, National Library of Ireland.
5. Stanley van der Ziel's annotated bibliography provides details of reviews of *The Barracks*, *Irish University Review* 35(1) (Spring/Summer 2005); further details are included in this author's *Outstaring Nature's Eye*, 34, n. 2.
6. Bruce Arnold, review of *The Barracks*, *Irish Times*, 23 February 1963.

Index